WHAT IF
GOD
WROTE YOUR
SHOPPING
LIST?

JAY PAYLEITNER

HARVEST HOUSE PUBLISHERS
EUGENE, OREGON

Cover design by Bryce Williamson

Cover photo © loops7; Timbenh/Getty Images

Published in association with the Steve Laube Agency, LLC, 24 W. Camelback Rd. A-635, Phoenix, Arizona 85013.

What If God Wrote Your Shopping List?
Copyright © 2019 by Jay Payleitner
Published by Harvest House Publishers
Eugene, Oregon 97408
www.harvesthousepublishers.com

ISBN 978-0-7369-7728-9 (pbk.)
ISBN 978-0-7369-7729-6 (eBook)

Library of Congress Cataloging-in-Publication Data

Names: Payleitner, Jay K., author.
Title: What if God wrote your shopping list? / Jay Payleitner.
Description: Eugene : Harvest House Publishers, 2019.
Identifiers: LCCN 2019011986 (print) | LCCN 2019013479 (ebook) | ISBN 9780736977296 (ebook) | ISBN 9780736977289 (pbk.)
Subjects: LCSH: Decision making--Religious aspects--Christianity. | Choice (Psychology)--Religious aspects--Christianity. | Values--Religious aspects--Christianity. | Consumption (Economics)--Religious aspects--Christianity.
Classification: LCC BV4509.5 (ebook) | LCC BV4509.5 .P39 2019 (print) | DDC 241/.68--dc23
LC record available at https://lccn.loc.gov/2019011986

Contents

About Stuff

I need more stuff. Lots and lots of stuff. I have empty cabinets and corners I need to fill with stuff. Stuff is the only thing that makes me happy. Stuff makes life worth living. Give me stuff. And don't stop giving me stuff.

Said no one ever.

Sure, stuff can be nice. But deep down you know stuff doesn't make dreams come true. In fact, stuff often distracts you from being your best self. So let's forget about acquiring lots of stuff and instead think about stuff you really need.

Like a Bible. That's something you literally need. You have one, right? If you don't, stop reading *this* book and get yourself a copy of *God's* book. Find a translation that works for you. Like the New International Version, or the New Living Translation, or the English Standard Version. Look up a few favorite verses and pick the translation that speaks to you.

And don't go cheap. Get a study Bible with a sturdy binding and plenty of footnotes, maps, charts, indexes, and cross-references.

Then what? What else might be on God's shopping list for your life? Excellent question. The answer is different for everybody.

Let's see. I'm pretty sure you already have most of your necessities:

- ✓ pair of jeans that fits
- ✓ working phone
- ✓ toothbrush
- ✓ ~~tuna boat~~
- ✓ way to get around town
- ✓ the ability to read

✓ time to yourself

✓ hope

✓ clean socks

Check, check, and check? That's good. This is stuff you need. If you don't have those things, please put them on your shopping list. Except the tuna boat. As you can see, that has been crossed out, which means you probably don't need it. Unless you're a tuna fisherman who needs a new boat.

Similarly, you may have noticed the contents page also features a few chapter titles that are crossed off. Don't skip those chapters. They represent stuff that probably *isn't* on God's shopping list.

Notice also that you can actually purchase some of these things, and others are not really for sale. That idea is an ongoing theme in this book. Many of the chapters include specific recommendations on things to buy. Some chapters spell out things you'll want to *consider* buying. And some chapters will challenge you to pursue ideas and relationships that have no price tag.

By the way, this book is a sequel to two other books. *What If God Wrote Your Bucket List?* invites you to imagine what you should do before you kick the bucket. *What If God Wrote Your To-Do List?* imagines slightly more urgent strategies for things to do before the sun sets or the seasons change.

This book, *What If God Wrote Your Shopping List?*, is really about prioritizing your pursuits in life. Will you mistakenly chase stuff that distracts and dishonors? Or will you invest in stuff that lasts for eternity, like community, keepsakes, and crowns?

I hope you'll regard these pages as more than a simple shopping list. Consider them your invitation to a noble quest.

The people who sell stuff never tell you that
the stuff that really matters isn't stuff.

JAY PAYLEITNER

Harvest Table

This chapter is really about fellowship, but that's not something you can actually purchase. So instead, let's put "large, inviting table with plenty of room for guests" on God's shopping list.

Flip through your Bible, and you may be surprised at how often the act of sharing a meal coincides with community building and inspired teaching. That includes Jesus's first miracle at the wedding in Cana, the Last Supper, the feast celebrating the return of the prodigal son, the miracle of the loaves and fish, and Jesus's dining with tax collectors and sinners.

The book of Acts specifically connects communal meals with three critical disciplines: teaching, fellowship, and prayer. Acts 2:42 says, "They devoted themselves to the apostles' teaching and to fellowship, to the breaking of bread and to prayer."

Look up that verse in context, and you'll see it's sandwiched between two other huge developments for the new church. In a single day, three thousand new converts are baptized. Then comes the meal. Shortly after that, "everyone was filled with awe at the many wonders and signs performed by the apostles" (Acts 2:43).

You probably had no idea that just breaking bread together could be part of such a world-changing turn of events.

All of which confirms the need to put a harvest table on your shopping list. In other words, a good-sized, sturdy, welcoming dining room table.

After moving into their first home, my son Randall and his bride, Rachel, had a butcher-block harvest table built to maximize the space in their dining room. It's a beautiful piece of furniture and so much more. That table has already seen scores of birthday parties, pumpkin-carving contests, board game tournaments, pre-Thanksgiving smorgasbords (aka Friendsgiving), and weekly fellowship meals.

In my home, for more than twenty Thanksgivings, I fashioned an eight-foot square table out of two laminated sheets of plywood. There was just enough space in our dining room to squeeze up to eighteen guests around the table. The conversation around and across the giant square table confirms the value of fellowship and the best ways to inspire it—good food, shared values, a sense of humor, and mutual respect.

No matter how big it is and no matter how many people are gathered, make your dining table a sacred place, a place of blessing. And as necessary, a place of brokenness, forgiveness, and welcoming strangers. Before partaking in any meal, join hands and give thanks to the one true provider. Applaud the meal preparers. Share stories of the day, the season, or the year. When a milk glass tumbles, don't make it a big deal.

If you gather with open hearts, there's a good chance your shared experience of breaking bread can even have healing powers. In even the best of families and communities, hard feelings and division can creep into relationships. For reasons either silly or serious. It's amazing how a long silence between two siblings or old friends can come to an end when one of them simply says, "Can you pass the potatoes?"

Checking the List

At the Last Supper, Jesus set in motion a series of events that changed the world. It started with washing feet and ended three days later with an empty tomb. At the table, he broke bread and challenged all of us, "Do this in remembrance of me."

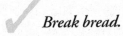 *Break bread.*

Mirror

You already have a mirror in your home. Probably several. That's a good thing. Mirrors can reveal critical truths.

Such as *I have spinach in my teeth.* Or *I need to trim my nose hairs.* Or *I need to party not quite so hard next weekend.* Seeing the frightening reflection of bloodshot eyes and a hangdog expression in the morning can make a compelling argument for you to make better decisions and come home at a decent hour in the future.

Mirrors are also valuable to assist you in looking your best. Not hours primping and judging and wishing for higher cheekbones or better hair. But doing what needs to be done—shaving, tweezing, brushing, applying just enough makeup—to get through the day with the right dose of confidence. With the added benefit of not scaring the dog or your neighbor. Think of those three to ten minutes in front of the bathroom mirror not as a burden but as a gift to the people you'll meet later that day.

(Plus, taking that time at home will keep your eyes on the road rather than applying mascara in your rearview mirror.)

But God needs you to have a nice, clear mirror for another reason. Especially in the morning, because he wants you to give yourself a little pep talk. It might go something like this:

- *"This is the day the LORD has made. [I] will rejoice and be glad in it"* (Psalm 118:24 NLT).

- *God has given me a gift from his great variety of spiritual gifts. I will use them well to serve others* (see 1 Peter 4:10).

- *I can live confidently knowing the Lord directs my steps and delights in every detail of my life* (see Psalm 37:23).

- *I have turned to the Lord, so the veil is removed, and I can see and reflect the glory of the Lord. And the Lord—who is the Spirit—is making me more and more like him, changing me into his glorious image* (see 2 Corinthians 3:16-18).

- *"The LORD will work out his plans for my life—for your faithful love, O LORD, endures forever. Don't abandon me, for you made me"* (Psalm 138:8 NLT).

- *"I am certain that God, who began the good work within [me], will continue his work until it is finally finished on the day when Christ Jesus returns"* (Philippians 1:6 NLT).

Notice that these pep talks are not telling you how great you are. Or perfect. Or self-sufficient. Like so much of Scripture, these verses serve as reminders that we are dependent on the Lord. He guides us. He empowers us. He pours out spiritual gifts into our lives so we can complete our mission and give him glory. Which is a pretty sweet deal for that face staring back at you. Don't you agree?

As you look in that mirror, there's one more amazing truth you may not have considered. God has always seen you as beautiful, but if you have been redeemed, you are covered with the righteousness of Christ because of the cross. The one ugly thing about you—your sin—has been washed away by his blood. That person in the mirror is a new creation.

Every time you look in the mirror, you would do well to make that your very first thought.

Checking the List

Have you noticed that what the world values is not always the opposite of what God values but often just a slightly distorted version? God makes all things beautiful, but the culture imposes its own obsessive version of beauty. God honors hard work, but we all know people who work so much their family and faith suffer. God invented sex, but the culture denies that it flows out of love and respect in a committed marriage relationship. God's shopping list would include all of us buying into his heavenly-minded perspective on beauty, work, and sex.

 See yourself as God sees you.

Lemonade Stand Lemonade

This item on God's shopping list is not something you can plan. But when God gives you the opportunity, don't miss it.

Make it a rule. When driving through a neighborhood and you happen upon a classic lemonade stand set up and manned by young entrepreneurs around middle school age, always stop and buy a glass of lemonade.

In general, we want to encourage this kind of behavior, right? Enterprise and self-actualization are traits we want young people to identify and develop.

Hopefully, the price is fair and the lemonade is cold and good quality. It usually is. At the site of this transaction, feel free to strike up a short conversation with the young businesspeople.

"How's business?"

"How's the return on your investment?"

"What do you plan to do with your profits?"

Treat them like professionals. Don't say "How cute." Don't tell them the lemonade is delicious if it isn't. If the product is lukewarm, recommend—one business person to another—that they invest in some ice cubes. Ideally, they count back your change properly. Which means not just giving you back a fistful of bills and coins but doing the math properly, presenting you with a total, repeating the amount of money received from you, and indicating how much you are getting back. If they do it right, feel free to say "Nice job" or "Pleasure doing business with you." If they get sloppy with the math or transaction, decide whether you want to make it a teachable moment.

Lemonade stands pop up most often in suburban neighborhoods. I don't seem to see as many today as I did years ago, which makes it even more critical that we stop and give them our business. Proper lemonade buying etiquette suggests you stop the car maybe twenty feet past the stand, exit your car slowly, smile, and say something friendly, like "What a welcome sight. I *am* feeling a bit parched today." Then wait for their sales pitch.

If you have a ten-year-old and live in the right kind of neighborhood—with light traffic and in-town speed limits—you would do well to encourage your son or daughter to set up a lemonade stand. Especially if it's a warm summer day and they are complaining that there's nothing to do. For safety and efficiency, it's a two-person job, so have them recruit a friend or sibling. Lend them the card table, pitcher, and cooler. But make sure they invest up front in the lemons, ice, and disposable cups. Or float them a loan. It's a business, after all.

If you are shouting, "Stranger danger!" be assured I'm aware of the cultural climate. Please allow your own good judgment to guide the way.

The rule to stop at lemonade stands extends to other avenues of young salesmanship as well. Of course, buy Girl Scout cookies and whatever is being sold by other organizations, like the Boy Scouts or Trail Life USA. When young people ring your doorbell, politely raising funds for a high school band trip to the Rose Bowl parade or a youth group mission trip to Appalachia, you will want to put in a reasonable order for whatever they're selling. If they have a snow shovel or rake in hand, offering to clear your walk or bag your leaves, that's even better. Be warned—if an older teen or young adult comes to your door with a slick sales pitch selling magazine subscriptions, be respectful, but exercise good judgment. The goal is to support local kids from your neighborhood and community.

The Bible endorses honest work, good stewardship, being a good neighbor, and mentoring the next generation. Lemons are not mentioned in the Bible, but there is a precedent regarding the value of being generous involving a cold drink: "If you give even a cup of cold water to one of the least of my followers, you will surely be rewarded" (Mathew 10:42 NLT).

Checking the List

Let your generous spirit, hope for the next generation, and thirst guide you. But if you have a dollar you can spare, please do stop at the next lemonade stand you see.

 Champion ambitious young people.

Swimming with a Dolphin

Planning a family trip to the Florida Keys, I came across several attractions featuring a chance to interact with dolphins. You could watch them perform from a distance. You could lean into the pool and pet them. Or for a hefty sum, you could swim with them. My initial instinct was *pet the dolphins.* I thought, *That would be so cool.* And it was the medium-price option. Not cheap, but not extravagant. When making decisions about budgeting, I typically seem to choose the middle option.

However, when I dialed the phone and pulled out my credit card, for some unexpected reason, I went for it all.

Over those few days in South Florida, my family walked the edge of the everglades, went snorkeling off a pontoon boat, climbed a lighthouse, and lay on the beach. But we all agree the highlight was swimming with the dolphin. Our own dolphin.

At the aquatic center, as they divided the guests into groups, we requested to be kept together. When they realized that my five kids were all in one family, they assigned us one trainer and one dolphin for the entire hour. Alec, Randy, Max, Isaac, and Rae Anne all had three turns with Stormy. They hugged and kissed her, they zipped alongside her on a dorsal tow, and they each got a high-speed "foot push" around the inlet. Rita and I just watched, cheered, and videoed. It was a total blast.

The point is that sometimes—not always—but sometimes we should bite the bullet and splurge. For our families. For our friends. Maybe just for ourselves.

Can you imagine these words coming out of your mouth? "Banana splits for everyone." "I'll take all three pairs." "Brunch is on me." "This Sunday afternoon we're going on a hot-air-balloon ride." "Got any seats on the fifty-yard line?" Not often, but once in a while, splurging is the right choice.

Having said that, frugality is usually the best choice. The Bible has much to say about being prudent and thoughtful when it comes to money.

- "The wise store up choice food and olive oil, but fools gulp theirs down" (Proverbs 21:20).

- "On the first day of each week, you should each put aside a portion of the money you have earned" (1 Corinthians 16:2 NLT).

- "The plans of the diligent lead to profit" (Proverbs 21:5).

- "Keep your lives free from the love of money and be content with what you have" (Hebrews 13:5).

- "If you have not been trustworthy in handling worldly wealth, who will trust you with true riches?" (Luke 16:11).

Don't be a glutton. Save regularly. Work hard. Be content. Invest wisely. These are all good principles to practice.

With that goal in mind, this chapter suggests that—if you can handle it—God would likely include the word "splurge" on your shopping list. Not to the point of gluttony or carelessness. But I think it's much easier to honor these biblical principles and be a good steward of God's generosity if you occasionally make the investment and go the extra mile.

So…splurge. And that might even include swimming with the dolphins.[1]

Checking the List

On the other hand, if you splurge all the time—almost never saying no to your whims and cravings—then I might suggest doing just the opposite. Take a purposeful fast from online shopping, catalog browsing, and outlet malls.

 Once in a while, splurge.

Rocking Chair

Anytime is a good time to sit in a rocking chair. A nice sturdy rocking chair is comfortable, soothing, focusing, maintenance-free, and affordable. Specifically, there are three times when sitting and rocking is especially well chosen and well timed.

1. In your first home. Furnishing first homes and apartments often means you're starting out with a wobbly kitchen table and a slightly worn, overstuffed armchair donated by family or friends. You're glad for those pieces. That table becomes a favorite location to spread out your homework, art projects, tax forms, newspapers, or work endeavors. You flop on that old armchair thousands of times with a book, comforter, or television remote.

But a solid wood rocking chair just might be your first financial investment in a piece of real furniture. It's handsome. It fits nicely in a corner. You can spill drinks on it with little or no damage. Guests like it. And you can pick one up for a couple hundred bucks or so. That's not cheap, but it's a purchase that says, "I'm an adult now. And I'm making my own way in this world."

The best part is that when a young person rocks, negativity is eased away. That rocking motion becomes a series of head nods and positive thoughts. *I'm going to move past the crud of today. I'm looking forward to a fresh start tomorrow. I wonder what God has for me in this next season.* Try it! It works!

2. *When you bring home a newborn.* Leaving the maternity ward, you're still in a kind of *What-are-we-doing?* daze. For new moms and dads, a rocking chair is the perfect place to hold your baby and get centered. Rocking an infant is often the time when new parents (especially first-time parents) begin to balance two kinds of prayers—prayers for the moment and prayers for the future.

You look down and see that perfect specimen of humanity (even if that little one is not perfect according to the health professionals). You pray they sleep soundly. You pray the dog, doorbell, or siblings don't wake them. You pray the diaper doesn't leak through. And you pray a moment of rest for yourself.

Simultaneously, you develop a new passion for praying for their future. It's a daring undertaking. You pray this small bundle of love will find his or her place in this world. You start to envision the uncertainty of what lies ahead, so you pray they make friends, learn to love, find a worthy husband or wife, and accept Christ into their life at an early age. You may even pray that someday they don't need you anymore.

Also, rocking a newborn, you start to sing. Even if you hate your voice. You can't help it. In almost every case, dads and moms will find themselves gently and sweetly singing lullabies, hymns, and rock 'n' roll classics. Blame it on the rocker.

3. *On the front porch.* Over your lifetime, you might own several houses featuring a variety of architectural designs. Please make sure the last house you own has a covered front porch with room for your rocking chair.

It's a cliché, but there are reasons older folks like to sit on the front porch and rock. The fresh air. Just enough "exercise" to keep the blood moving. The elevated vantage point to see what's going on in the world. And a chance to meet and greet visitors as soon as they walk up the front path.

With that thought, let's all look forward to being that senior citizen who rocks, prays, loves, remembers back, looks ahead with a sense of gratitude, and humbly shares wisdom with all we meet.

Take this shopping list item to heart, and you may discover that time spent in a good rocking chair will even help you fulfill the biblical admonition of Philippians 4:8: "Whatever is true, whatever is noble, whatever is right, whatever is pure, whatever is lovely, whatever is admirable—if anything is excellent or praiseworthy—think about such things."

Checking the List

There's a good chance your first rocker in your first apartment could be the same one that ends up on your front porch decades from now. So make sure it's well built and well loved. It might even be one you inherit from your grandmother. Wouldn't that be legendary and legacy building?

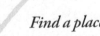 *Find a place to rock on.*

Red-Letter Bible

Make sure at least one of the Bibles in your home is a red-letter edition. It's remarkable to peruse through those editions and let the highlighted words speak directly to your heart. In those special editions, the publisher prints the words spoken by Jesus in red ink.

Every word of Scripture is "God-breathed and is useful for teaching, rebuking, correcting and training in righteousness" (2 Timothy 3:16), yet the words printed in red ink seem to take the privilege and immediate benefits of reading the Bible one step further. We imagine Jesus, the Son of God, walking right here on the same dusty earth on which we trudge and speaking those highlighted words.

Flipping through the Gospels, of course, is where you find most of the red ink. But you will find a sprinkling of red occasionally in the rest of the New Testament, including Acts, 1 Corinthians, 2 Corinthians, and 1 Timothy.

The first three chapters of Revelation include a long passage that Jesus will speak at his second coming, sounding like a great trumpet. Revelation 22:20 gives us the final red letters in the Bible: "Yes, I am coming soon."

Focusing on the words of Christ in the Gospels, we often read direct commands: "Come, follow me" (Mark 1:17), "Honor your father and mother" (Matthew 15:4), and "Take and eat; this is my body" (Matthew 26:26). We like that. When it comes to God's Son, we appreciate specific instructions. It takes out the guesswork.

Even better than commands are exhortations to do things we desperately want and need to do. The best example is Matthew 6:9, where Jesus clearly states, "This, then, is how you should pray."

What comes next—still in red ink—is commonly referred to as the Lord's Prayer. In the New International Version, it's only sixty-four words, but not surprisingly, it covers everything you really need to consider when praying to God. Biblical scholars could spend countless days considering the meaning of each phrase, but let's see what we can glean in just a page or so.

"Our Father in heaven." The Creator of the universe wants a Father-child relationship with each of us. He's real. And he's living in a place of eternal glory.

"Hallowed be your name." Even God's name is set apart. Holy. Just mentioning his name unleashes unstoppable power.

"Your kingdom come, your will be done." Those are true statements. God reigns. God's will triumphs. But they are also prayer requests. We are asking God to send his Son back for his triumphant return—soon. And we are surrendering our will for his. He knows what's best for us anyway.

"On earth as it is in heaven." These are two different places, but God is in control of both. Humans can't even begin to understand how the world and universe work. There's no way we can grasp the awesomeness of heaven.

"Give us today our daily bread." This is straightforward—except it's not just bread, and it's not just daily. God supplies all our needs. From oxygen to sunlight to the way our brains turn squiggly lines printed on the pages of this book into ideas on how God wants us to invest our resources. How it all works together is God's gift to us.

"Forgive us our debts, as we also have forgiven our debtors." This could be considered the centerpiece of the gospel. We must acknowledge our brokenness and ask for God's forgiveness. It's the blood of Christ that

washes away our sins. If we understand the critical nature and power of forgiveness, we will also follow God's example. But our job is easier. All we must do is forgive those who have wronged us, one person at a time. We can't begin to compare that to God's promise to forgive all the sins of all the people throughout history who believe and trust in him.

"And lead us not into temptation, but deliver us from the evil one." To be clear, God would never lead us into temptation. But he did give us free will, which means he allows us to be tempted and we need to ask him to save us from ourselves. The second part pinpoints the urgency. Satan is real, and we can't face him alone.

"For yours is the kingdom and the power and the glory forever." We've come full circle now. He's our Father in heaven, and his glory will last forever. He is the Alpha and the Omega.

"Amen." Amen.

If you grew up in a home that rattled off the Lord's Prayer in eleven seconds or less, try slowing it down. There's so much to be considered.

If the Lord's Prayer is not part of your regular prayer arsenal, you're missing out. If the words of Jesus don't touch your heart, you'll want to spend some real time considering who he is and what he's saying. No shopping necessary.[2]

Checking the List

Most homes in America have a Bible. You may have several. Some homes have more than a dozen. That's all well and good, but it's only step one. If it's been a while since you've dusted off your Bible, you may be wondering where to start. Pick a Gospel and read the true story of Jesus of Nazareth. And if you're a regular Bible reader, maybe it's time to spend a season on his specific instructions to you.

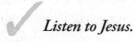 **Listen to Jesus.**

Library Card

I live in a city recently voted by *Family Circle* magazine to be the best place in America to raise a family. I couldn't agree more. St. Charles, Illinois, has served my family well. But it's not cheap.

My city real estate tax bill is high. And it's eye-opening to look at the breakdown of how those thousands and thousands of dollars are distributed. There are seven categories.

A huge majority chunk goes to schools. After that—in descending order—are the park district, city (police, fire, and public works), local community college, county, library, and forest preserve.

Every city is different, but there's a good chance you are also directly or indirectly paying property taxes that cover a similar array of services. Even if you rent, of course, your landlord is still forking over big dollars every year.

Reading the fine print on my annual statement, I see that my family—and every family in my neighborhood—is paying hundreds of dollars toward the local public library. Is that something you think about? You should. For one reason, if you're paying for something, you might as well use it. But more than that, your local library is a ready resource for more information, technology, street smarts, and entertainment than most people imagine.

All that to say, I am stunned to report that I have neighbors who don't own a library card. They're already paying for the books, staff, building, computers, magazines, newspapers, programs, and upkeep. And these neighbors have never set foot in the building.

If you fall into this category, then this is a no-brainer. Actually, it's a brain-gainer. Go get your library card. Then carve out a couple hours to walk the stacks, flip through some magazines, and get an overview of the technology that you've already helped pay for.

What stage of life are you in? What are your hobbies? Planning a vacation? Changing careers? Curious about your ancestry? Interested in local, national, or world history? Starting a business? Filing for bankruptcy? Writing your memoirs? Want to know more about bigfoot, volcanoes, single-celled organisms, world religions, aluminum recycling, or the origin of the universe?

Answers are right there in the big brick building close to the center of town. Navigating the Dewey decimal system, you'll want to use some discernment in separating trustworthy facts from questionable claims. But you get the idea. Like your internet excursions, your time in the library can be a rabbit trail of discovery, taking you from one idea to the next until your brain is spinning.

Then there are the books that really can't be compared to anything you'll find on a computer screen. Biographies. Memoirs. Histories. Books sorting out theological questions and philosophical conundrums. And of course, all kind of fiction—science, historical, Westerns, gothic, mysteries, thrillers, swashbucklers, and romance.

Quite a few library books have more than words. Open a book and your imagination to full-color pages of fine art, sketches, graphic-novel panels, photography, blueprints, formulas, comics, and maps.

A word of warning: Libraries aren't as quiet as they used to be. In general, people aren't shouting across rooms, and librarians will expect you to take cell phone conversations outside. But you will no longer find spinster librarians aggressively shushing the patrons. And that's mostly okay. Personally, I make sure all my library-based conversations are short and whispered. But not everyone abides by those antiquated rules. Still, I am confident you will find your library to be a retreat and respite from the fast-paced outside world.

If you're already a regular library devotee, I recommend you introduce a neighbor or child to the joys of walking through the doors and exploring the building. And the world.

If you live in a library district, you don't have to put a library card on your shopping list. You already paid for it. (Except perhaps for a small processing fee.) All you have to do is walk in and ask. Every librarian I've ever met loves welcoming new readers.

Checking the List

Consider this quote from the associate publisher of a major Christian publishing house: "In a world of myriad media options, there are now people who read books and people who don't. Book readers are better off" (Randall Payleitner).

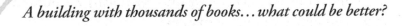 *A building with thousands of books…what could be better?*

World Map Shower Curtain

Several years back, this item appeared on a Payleitner family shopping list: "shower curtain for the boys' bathroom." We were seeking nothing fancy or extraordinary. Our four boys were past the age of teddy bears and cartoon monkeys, so the goal was to find something that would keep the water off the bathroom floor and not clash with the wallpaper.

What we ended up purchasing turned out to be a fantastic, mind-expanding addition to their educational and spiritual well-being.

We found it at Bed Bath & Beyond. For less than twenty bucks. A clear shower curtain with a visual representation of all 190-plus countries on the planet. It was an easy and obvious purchase. Suddenly, every shower became a geography lesson. While they lathered and rinsed, they noticed how three fairly large western states bordered the Pacific Ocean and fourteen smaller states bordered the Atlantic. They identified for themselves the boot of Italy, the expanse of the former Soviet Union, the Mediterranean and Red Seas, and the islands of Iceland, Ireland, Madagascar, Cuba, Tasmania, and Indonesia. The idea of continental drift started to make sense as they saw how Africa seems like it could have once fit into the Caribbean. Most importantly, the six-foot-wide shower curtain served as visual proof that a world exists beyond their own neighborhood.

That's a concept we all need to grasp. If that lesson starts with a colorful shower curtain, that's not a bad thing. The question is, How do we use this new information?

On God's shopping list is for each of us to develop a heart for people in every corner of the earth. According to the gospel of Matthew, Jesus's final instruction to his followers was to "go and make disciples of all nations" (Matthew 28:19-20). That outreach begins with our families, neighborhood, and community. But we also have a responsibility to move beyond our small sphere of influence and outside our comfort zone.

For some that means praying intentionally for lost people in faraway places you will never visit in this life. For others that might mean packing up your belongings and moving to the other side of the world to share the gospel with people who live on one of those brightly colored spots on your shower curtain.

Investing our hearts, minds, and resources in those lives is easier than ever. Technology and instant communication can make us aware of their hopes, dreams, needs, and gifts and even enable us to share in their day-to-day experiences. Ministries like Voice of the Martyrs, Prison Fellowship, and Bible League know how to cut through the bureaucracies to deliver truth and love in tangible ways. Those kinds of trusted, established ministries are always looking for individuals like you with whom to partner.

As our minds attempt to grasp the idea of close to eight billion people living in 190 countries, a humility should probably wash over each of us. In one sense, we're each just a speck of dust. But God's love gives us purpose. His heart is big enough to love you, me, and every one of our neighbors on the planet. And he wants us to do the same.

I'm not sure if a multicolored world map shower curtain fits into the decor of your master bathroom. In fact, it probably doesn't. Maybe you don't even have a shower. But you do have room in your home for a globe, wall map, or world atlas. Next time you start to feel like the world revolves around you, spin that globe, study that map, or flip through that atlas.

If you start to feel small, that's okay. Just remember you have the ability and responsibility to plug into the power that created not just the world but the entire universe.

Checking the List

Please don't race to Jakarta or Mahajanga next week. (Unless God is giving you an amazingly clear call.) But do take a purposeful step toward becoming a true world Christian. Taking a short-term mission trip or supporting a missionary family will deepen your understanding of how God sees the world and how you can make a difference, right where you are.

 *God so loves the world.*

The Newest Smartphone on the Day It Comes Out

I t's definitely cool to be the first person in your circle of friends to own the latest tech gadget. There's even an enviable adulation connected with camping overnight or waiting in line outside a store for hours to be an early adopter. You might say that ordeal scores a bit of a wow factor.

And when a new iPhone comes out, the price is well documented in the media. So not only can you impress your friends, colleagues, and enemies with your physical tenacity to stand in line, but you are also letting them know that your lifestyle is not limited by your cash flow or your credit card balance.

What's more, there's a daredevil prestige about being the test market for a new product. With your day-of-release purchase, you are telling the tech company and the world that you are willing to be a sort of guinea pig. In their rush to market, companies like Apple, Samsung, or Lenovo pretty much expect some bugs to emerge in the first few months of actual customer usage. They are counting on you, a "lighthouse customer," to identify product flaws but not whine too much about them. After all, you knew what you were getting into.

So those are three reasons right there to *not* include the newest smartphone on your shopping list. Wasting time waiting for the doors to open. Paying top dollar. Presumed malfunctions.

On the other hand, it's probably okay for certain people in certain situations to ignore the commonsense approach to smartphones and choose to be an early adopter.

My son Randall is a case in point. The year was 2007. Randall was single, he had a decent income and no debt, and he was already appreciative of Apple products and Apple service. His current phone contract was up. And he knew his friends would be jealous.

So. On the *second* day the original iPhone was available in Chicago, he bought one. He stood in line behind just five people. He paid full price. And had no regrets.

If you recall, that first generation iPhone was quite a stunning achievement. Apple CEO Steve Jobs introduced it as a combination of three devices: a "widescreen iPod with touch controls," a "revolutionary mobile phone," and a "breakthrough internet communicator." For most users, it was the first time using a touchscreen, the first time you could swipe left or right to see photos, and the first time you could zoom in on an image using two fingers. All stuff that is old news with current smartphones.

But in 2007, those features were stunning. Randall recalls people on public transportation asking if they could hold it for just a moment, and he let them. Less than a week after his purchase, Randall held his annual Third of July party, and I nervously tested his new gadget. Its capabilities were beyond anything I had imagined up to that point.

Randall survived his role as early adopter. There wasn't much downside, and he chose to *not* stand in line for any future smartphone releases. As a matter of fact, just to prove he wasn't addicted to the latest technology, when his original iPhone contract ran out, he went back to a flip phone for a year or two. He has since returned to the iPhone flock.

Like so many of the shopping list items in this book, when it comes to acquiring the latest and greatest technology, the decision is yours. If

you're working in Silicon Valley or some other tech arena, you probably need to stay on the cutting edge. If you've done your research and
you're confident a piece of high-tech gear can save you time, make you
more efficient, or broaden your impact in the world, then go for it. If
you've saved up a few hundred bucks by cutting back on impulse buying for several months, then enjoy your splurge.

But if you find yourself shivering outside an Apple store with a
hundred scary-looking people about to max out your credit card on
a fancy phone that will likely be prone to malfunction, then step out
of that line and do a reality check. *Do I need it? Can I afford it? What's
my real motivation? Should I wait a few months and see if it's still on my
shopping list?*

Checking the List

Just because it's available doesn't mean you have to have it, right?
Maybe the biggest clue is this: If half the population simply must have
it, then maybe it's time be countercultural and simply say, "No, thanks.
I can wait."

 ***Saying no to the latest and greatest product helps you
reaffirm that you are more than your stuff.***

Alarm Clock

I confess, this must-have item on God's shopping list feels optional for me. That's probably not a good thing.

The arc of my writing career has totally messed up my sleep patterns, and the result is that I work and sleep crazy hours. I often get an inspiration for a chapter or script in the middle of the night and stumble to my keyboard before the idea gets lost between dreams. Some of my best ideas have been captured—or lost forever—depending on whether I have the diligence to climb out of bed. When I do make it down the stairs to my office, I may sit at my desk undistracted for two or three hours before going back to bed. If I've had a productive late-night writing session, you certainly can't blame me for not honoring a six a.m. alarm.

I also take a twenty- to thirty-minute nap at three o'clock most afternoons.

Just about the only time I need an alarm clock is Fridays, when I get up at the crack of dawn for my small group. Other times might be if Rita and I are headed out the door together at an early hour, but I can always count on her to gently and lovingly nudge me awake. (Or something like that.) When I'm on the road, I request a wake-up call from the front desk.

All that to say, typically I wait until I wake up to wake up. And that does not require an alarm clock. Which means I am not the best person in the world to speak to the advantages of intentionally rising early and greeting the day. Thankfully, there is a much greater authority to guide us in that area: God's Word.

Allow me to recognize a few biblical characters who endorse the idea of waking early. Especially to meet with God.

In Genesis 28, Jacob makes a bed out of rocks and dreams of his role as the wellspring of God's people. How and when does he mark the occasion? "Early the next morning Jacob took the stone he had placed under his head and set it up as a pillar and poured oil on top of it" (Genesis 28:18).

In 1 Samuel, Hannah would give birth to Israel's greatest judge. How and when was Samuel conceived? "Early the next morning they arose and worshiped before the Lord and then went back to their home at Ramah. Elkanah made love to his wife Hannah, and the Lord remembered her" (1 Samuel 1:19).

In 2 Chronicles, Hezekiah leads a revival that begins with the purification of the temple. How and when does he get ready for the next step, sacrificing seven bulls, rams, lambs, and goats? "Early the next morning King Hezekiah gathered the city officials together and went up to the temple of the LORD" (2 Chronicles 29:20).

In the Psalms, David gets up while it's still dark to seek answers from God: "I rise before dawn and cry for help; I have put my hope in your word" (119:147).

Jesus modeled it best: "Very early in the morning, while it was still dark, Jesus got up, left the house and went off to a solitary place, where he prayed" (Mark 1:35).

So do you have an alarm clock? What if you set it twenty minutes earlier? What if you didn't slap that snooze alarm three or four times? What if you placed the alarm clock on the other side of the room so it forced you to get out of bed? What if you met with God for fifteen soul-satisfying minutes before beginning your day?

This is not a new idea. You've heard it before. Perhaps you've even gone through a significant season during which you prayed, read Scriptures, and journaled almost every morning. Remember how sweet that was? Why did you stop? Because life got in the way, right?

If you need to buy a new alarm clock to start or restart this habit, go for it. You can certainly find one for under twenty bucks. Or just set your smartphone for that desired time, and it will be with you wherever you go, even changing time zones as you crisscross the country.

What are the instant benefits of taking that first fifteen minutes of your day to spend time with God? Some are obvious. A fresh start to the day. Fewer distractions from family and other life responsibilities. The bookmark in your Bible keeps moving, one chapter or a few verses at a time. Truths uncovered in the morning will stay with you all day long.

Some benefits are less obvious. You may sleep better knowing you are not in charge of your day, God is. You'll have a grunt-free response for the first person who greets you in the morning. God may send a few bonus angels your way to protect you during the day. You may develop a more regular daily routine, including an earlier bedtime and a light exercise regime.

But really, the reason to acquire and set an alarm clock twenty minutes earlier every day is that God wants to spend time with you. That's right. The Creator of the universe wants to hang out with just you for a few minutes before you start your day. He wants you to find satisfaction in the truest thing about you—his unfailing love for you. "Satisfy us in the morning with your unfailing love, that we may sing for joy and be glad all our days" (Psalm 90:14).

Checking the List

Again, doing daily morning devotions is not a new idea. But it's so obvious that those few minutes of lost sleep can lead to a dramatic, positive difference for your entire day, week, and life. And if you are already faithfully setting that early alarm day after day, I salute you.

 Do daily morning devotions. Start tomorrow.

Art Supplies

If you're the kind of person who sometimes says, "I have no creative ability," please stop.

Maybe you're not a painter, sculptor, illustrator, or graphic designer. But what about the other arts? Maybe you've got undiscovered gifts as a musician, dancer, poet, novelist, playwright, actor, singer, or fashion designer.

Taking it a step further, might you see yourself as a chef, comedian, floral arranger, jewelry maker, cartoonist, set designer, landscape architect, woodworker, seamstress, calligrapher, web designer, video game designer, photographer, storyteller, puppeteer, graffiti tagger, choreographer, tattoo artist, mime, woodworker, welder, copywriter, or technical writer?

You can see how the terms "artist" or "creative person" can be defined in broader terms than simply visual arts. Sure, that building in the nearest big city labeled "art institute" is mostly filled with paintings and sculptures, but inspiring artistry most certainly exists beyond those walls. Creativity flourishes among men and women of science, philosophy, education, engineering, and commerce. Being a parent certainly demands ingenuity, imagination, and resourcefulness.

Make no mistake—you are creative.

Genesis 1:27 tells us, "God created mankind in his own image, in the image of God he created them." There's much packed in those words. They describe God as a Creator and reveal that humans are made in the image of God. Which means we must also have the gift to create. All of us.

What's more, you have a responsibility to harvest those creative gifts and use them to point people to the Creator.

So what does all this mean for your shopping list? Every individual is different, but you might start by asking, "How would I invest $200 or less to start exploring my creative side?" With that question, did some tool or process instantly come to mind? Perhaps woodcarving tools, graphic design software, a sewing machine, a camera, or an acetylene torch. Did you imagine yourself standing on a stage or pounding on a keyboard?

To trigger your dormant artistic hobby or career, a trip to the library or an evening browsing innovative websites might be in order. You may stumble across an entire new genre of art that didn't exist last time you looked. Something like graphic novels, music scoring for video games, anamorphosis, projection mapping, or 3-D laser design.

Take a class or seek out a creative circle of artists or authors. It could be time to finally get that piano tuned or pull out that set of oil paints in the back of your closet. Talk to your local artist guild, theater troupe, or barbershop quartet chapter. Your church or another local church body may have a creative arts team that welcomes volunteers.

Taking a step back, this chapter is not telling you to quit your job to be a starving artist. It's also not intended to heap on piles of guilt because you've been ignoring your gifts. The point is to consider leaving your comfort zone and spread your creative wings.

Don't let the naysayers, penny pinchers, or accidental killjoys distract you. A brief story from my own youth may help you escape a common trap for would-be creatives.

To their credit, my mom and dad recognized that I might have a flicker of artistic talent. One Christmas, they gave me an art studio in a box, complete with real oil paints, watercolors, pastel chalks, pencils, sketchpads, assorted brushes, mixing trays, and sharpeners. It was awesome. I remember it well because I studied it for hours on end. I looked at it. I imagined all I would create with it. But I never actually used it. I was afraid to.

The gift itself was encouraging, but their words that Christmas morning unintentionally snuffed out any creative spark. They said, "Now, don't waste it." With that admonition echoing in the back of my head, I dutifully committed to preserving those precious paints and brushes until I could use them properly.

My parents could have said, "Have fun. Experiment. When you run out, we'll get more." Words like that may have inspired me to take risks, explore my gifts, and if some technique didn't work, simply start again. Instead, those magnificent paints and pastels went untested. Years later, I came across them completely dried up. Ironically, they had been wasted along with my potential as a visual artist.

Let me be clear—there's no remorse. God had other plans for me, and I found other creative outlets. Most notably, stringing words together to challenge and entertain readers and audiences.

Worth noting, my parents, who were raised in the Great Depression, were quite accurate with their words. Resources shouldn't be wasted. But what my folks didn't realize is that our most valuable resources are not tangible materials such as paint, paper, clay, wood, film, or canvas. Our greatest resources are the personal gifts and talents God has given each one of us.

Uncovering and fully using those abilities would be my prayer for you. If this chapter inspires that kind of response, please send me a sample, photo, review, or invitation to a gallery show of your work.

Checking the List

As you explore your creative side, don't be one of those artists constantly agonizing over your craft. Set goals. Invest some of your time and your imagination. Try new ideas. Study the masters. Expect moments of frustration as well as inspiration. If a piece of your art doesn't turn out exactly as you hoped, that doesn't mean it's not valuable or worthwhile. Just the opposite! That means you're one step closer to making something you imagine come to life.

 Reflect the Creator in your own creativity.

Stuff with Scripture

Owning posters, plaques, coffee mugs, bumper stickers, and screensavers that feature quotes from Scripture does not make you a better person than your neighbor. You can plaster your walls with Christian-themed artwork and walk around with Bible passages on your T-shirt. You can even blast contemporary Christian music from your cubicle. But really, how you live your life—your actions—will reflect whether you've surrendered your life to Jesus.

Still, I suggest that God's shopping list for your life includes "stuff with Scripture." Part of it goes back to the Old Testament strategy of immersing yourself and your family in God's laws. In Deuteronomy 5, Moses recounts the Ten Commandments and spells out some of the consequences for being disobedient. The next chapter clearly recommends strategies for knowing and understanding God's laws.

> These commandments that I give you today are to be on your hearts. Impress them on your children. Talk about them when you sit at home and when you walk along the road, when you lie down and when you get up. Tie them as symbols on your hands and bind them on your foreheads. Write them on the doorframes of your houses and on your gates (Deuteronomy 6:6-9).

Translating Old Testament instructions to the twenty-first century is sometimes tricky, but this doesn't seem too difficult or outrageous. Let's start with what Moses seems to be suggesting. We need to remember, talk about, and display God's commands during the routines of life. Probably don't spray paint "John 3:16" on your garage door, but words of Scripture should literally be heard and seen around our homes. Also, I'm pretty sure that "tie them as symbols on your hands" and "bind them on your foreheads" do not translate as getting a Bible verse tattooed on your forearm or forehead. A better application of Moses's words might be to wear a simple gold bracelet engraved with your favorite verse.

Intentionally posting prayers or Scripture around your home is a solid idea. Without preaching, you're letting your family and any visitor know where your heart lies. Plus, you're holding yourself to the biblical standard as well.

For example, if you have Romans 12:18 framed in your living space proclaiming, "If it is possible, as far as it depends on you, live at peace with everyone," then there's a chance you might be a bit slower to anger. There are no guarantees—it's not magic—but I think that's fair to say.

With that in mind, let's take a stroll around Jay and Rita's house and see what we find.

In my office, biblical quotes are taped, nailed, and push-pinned all over the cluttered walls and bulletin board. My favorite is a small card with a graphic image that says, "I will not forget you! See, I have engraved you on the palms of my hands" (Isaiah 49:15-16).

Anyone walking in our front door immediately sees a cross-stitch by Rita with a farm scene and the inscription "To everything there is a season, a time for every purpose under heaven" (Ecclesiastes 3:1 NKJV).

Around the corner is a framed poster that asks, "What If He Is Who He Says He Is?" and the answer to that question is presented through fourteen passages of Scripture.

In the hallway upstairs, you can read "Lord—my hope is in You" (from Psalm 39:7) and also "I am the light of the world" (John 8:12).

In Rita's office is a framed print of Jeremiah 29:7 (NLV) that helps ground her noble efforts as an alderman in our city: "Work for the well-being of the city where I have sent you to and pray to the Lord for this. For if it is well with the city you live in, it will be well with you."

On the fridge is a magnet that reads, "With God all things are possible" (Matthew 19:26).

In my walk-around, I also noticed a plaque that says, "Love you to the moon and back," but I don't think that's from Scripture.

So that's a brief overview of the Payleitner walls and other decor. Even a casual observer can't miss the idea that we think God is real and worthy of praise. I can think back on quite a few fascinating and rewarding conversations, debates, and heart-to-heart talks that have taken place in my home that started with a visitor noticing a poster, plaque, or piece of framed artwork. Some of which ended with a small group of us joined in prayer.

Some say, "If only these walls could talk." As it turns out, they can.[3]

Checking the List

When people walk into your home or into your life, they should know fairly soon that your values are shaped by a relationship with Christ. Posters, paintings, and other wall hangings are not going to save the world. But surrounding yourself with words and objects that remind you of what's important is one way you can stay rooted in your faith. And they may open doors to sharing that faith with others.

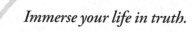 *Immerse your life in truth.*

Big League Scorecard

Here's a chapter for baseball fans. Specifically about your shopping list when you go see your favorite team play at your favorite ballpark.

If you're a true fan with a favorite player, you should know that an MLB regulation jersey made by Majestic will feature durable material, authentic colors, and sewn-on patches. No matter where you buy it, it's going to cost between $120 and $150, so you might as well buy it at the ballpark. They'll have a great selection, and you can tell people, "I bought it at Fenway" or Busch Stadium or wherever your fave team plays. Plus, at the ballpark, you'll know you're not getting an imitation knockoff jersey. Of course, with that kind of price tag, don't buy a jersey on a whim. If it's the right thing to buy for the right occasion, you'll know.

On the other hand, other fan apparel—T-shirts, sweatshirts, tank tops, caps, floppy hats—come in a wide range of quality and prices. Just go with your gut.

A word about noisemakers: They're not compatible with baseball. Especially those horrible inflatable thunder sticks. If you feel so compelled, you can clack them together at a football game where competitive tactics include bullet passes, long bombs, shotgun formations, and blitzes. But the cacophony of thunder sticks has no business at a game whose object is to be "safe at home." Just as bad are cowbells and vuvuzela horns. The last thing a baseball game needs is more cowbell.

Also, please don't buy foam fingers—they're ridiculous. In fact, most souvenirs that you don't wear are a waste of money and end up cluttering your shelves and drawers at home. The rare exception is an official league baseball with autographs collected by you or a family member. That's cool. Even cooler if it's a foul ball or home run you caught yourself.

Beyond those recommendations by this lifelong fan, I do have one mandatory purchase for you to make at each major league game you attend. Please *do* buy a scorecard and pencil. Especially if you are accompanying a youngster who is still learning the complexities and nuances of the great American pastime.

I'm thinking back to the annual Payleitner pilgrimage to the shrine at Clark and Addison. Growing up, my dad made sure we made it to at least one Chicago Cubs doubleheader every summer. One memorable outing occurred when I was about nine years old.

One of the great traditions for my brother and me was filling out our own scorecards with freshly sharpened Cubs pencils purchased from one of the vendors just inside the Wrigley Field turnstiles. In the 1960s, the scorecards were a quarter and the pencils were a dime. We never asked our dad for anything else. We knew the scorecard and pencil were our souvenirs. And those were enough.

About the second inning, tragedy struck. My pencil lead broke. Of course, I could sharpen it at home, but how was I going to complete my traditional duties filling in those tiny squares with initials like K, BB, FO7, HR, 4-6-3, and HBP? I couldn't ask for another pencil, could I?

I showed the unusable writing utensil to my dad, and he didn't miss a beat. He took it and within twenty seconds handed it back, sharpened and ready for the next batter. You may be able to guess what he did. To an adult, it may seem obvious. But to this nine-year-old, scraping that pencil at just the right angle with just the right pressure against the concrete floor of the grandstand was nothing short of brilliant. My dad was a genius!

Is "big league scorecard" really on God's shopping list for you? If you're a true baseball fan, sure. Otherwise, maybe not. Still, I hope the lesson is clear: Be intentional with souvenir shopping. Don't get things that are loud, expensive, breakable, or too big to carry home. Do consider souvenirs that are interactive, memorable, budget friendly, and likely to take a place of honor at home.

Memories from my youth fuel this recommendation. I trust memories of your own youth can lead you to add to your shopping list a meaningful souvenir or other memorabilia you will cherish for years to come.

Checking the List

Memories from your childhood can be a mixed bag. We can all recall grand victories, heartbreaking losses, warm fuzzies, challenges overcome, and some moments of true fear and desperation. Like a drawer full of souvenirs, hang on to those precious memories that bring a smile or a sense of wonder. Let go of all the others. That's not easy perhaps. But that's God desire for you. He puts the past in the past and has great plans for your future. Revelation 21:4 (NLT) promises, "He will wipe every tear from their eyes, and there will be no more death or sorrow or crying or pain. All these things are gone forever."

 You can't put a price tag on fond memories.

Disposable Serving Trays

Over the years, Rita has made—and I have delivered—quite a few meals for families who are hurting or overwhelmed during a season of life. It could be the exhausting season when a new baby comes home from the hospital—especially when two or three older siblings need to not feel forgotten. It could be when several members of a family seem to be living at the hospital, sitting bedside with a hurting loved one, and fast-food meals and takeout pizza are getting real old, real fast.

From making those deliveries, I know that a home-cooked meal delivered at about 5:45 p.m. can be quite a spectacular and welcome gesture.

I also know that no matter how many meals we send, Rita and I will never come close to preparing and delivering as many meals as we have received. After the birth of each of our five kids, during some of our busy days with foster babies, and a few other times when life challenges arose, someone would knock on the door and drop off a hot dish, some kind of salad, and a dessert as well! Chicken casserole, beef stew, pork chops, and lasagna come to mind. Those two or three meals during a stress-filled week were just enough to make life easier and impart the love of a community in a tangible way.

Whether it's well organized by the staff or magically happens by word of mouth, I am pretty sure that almost every established church in the country has some kind of "meals ministry." Often it flies completely under the radar. Only those who serve or are served know about it. Frankly, that kind of selfless caring is one of the great reasons to belong to a church family.

At one time, I believed we were frequent recipients of these love gifts because Rita was such a nice person. She is. But it turns out, meal ministries are all about just giving for the sake of giving. Loving because it's the right thing to do. Meeting real needs in the name of Jesus.

So what does this mean for God's shopping list for you? Well, if you have the gift of service and can make at least one decent casserole, insert yourself in that circle of volunteers who make and deliver meals to families and individuals in need. Some evenings you might be delivering to a longtime friend. Even better, some evenings it's a stranger who becomes a friend. Make sure your shopping list includes some fresh protein, veggies, and the ingredients to your favorite cookie recipe. Even as I type this, I chuckle because the Payleitner family often ate well when Rita was making those meals-to-go. She would just double the recipe to feed two families. On the other hand, sometimes the kids and I had to scrounge up leftovers because Rita had just enough resources to prepare the meal I would deliver.

For the record, she insisted I do the delivery. It was mostly fun. Sometimes hard. And I never stayed more than sixty seconds. Ring the doorbell, smile big, drop off a couple shopping bags, wish them well, and skedaddle home. Sometimes the recipients were so overwhelmed, they forgot to say thank you. That proves the value of the ministry.

One thing worth passing on is this *absolute meal ministry principle* from Rita: Always deliver food and beverages in containers that do not have to be returned. She recommends aluminum pans and plastic jugs. Make the entire meal disposable. Don't burden the already burdened family with the responsibility to track, wash, and return casserole dishes, cake pans, Tupperware, and pitchers.

I know this is critical because right now our kitchen cupboards contain at least one casserole dish and three or four Tupperware containers from meals delivered to our home long ago, even years ago. In the hubbub of life, we don't even know where they came from.

What if making and delivering meals just isn't your thing? The basic principles still apply. Invest your time, talent, and treasure in a ministry that might be under the radar. One that meets the real needs of real people. Sometimes strangers. Raise your hand and be part of a handyman ministry for single moms and seniors. Visit shut-ins and nursing homes. Do couples counseling. Career counseling. Financial planning. Community gardens for free vegetable distribution. Mentoring. Prison ministry. Or just make sure that your neighbors' snow gets shoveled or grass gets mowed when the need arises.

Under-the-radar ministry. Sorry, there's no glory. At least not on this side of heaven.

Checking the List

If you invest in an under-the-radar ministry, you should know that it's uncomfortable for some people to take charity. I recommend you let them off the hook. Say things like, "I needed the exercise" or "It's my pleasure" or "So many people have helped me over the years—I'm grateful I get a chance to give back." Finish the task and leave with just a hint of mystery, like a guardian angel. They may not know your name, but they'll never forget your gesture.

 When you give, make your gift easy to receive.

Wedding Rings

The only piece of jewelry I wear is my wedding ring. In the bottom of my sock drawer, I could probably find a tie tack I haven't worn in decades and a pair of cuff links I inherited from my dad. That's the extent of my personal jewelry collection.

Of course, I know guys can wear other jewelry. A neck chain, service ring, dog tags, bracelets, or even earrings. But that's not my style. Watches—including pocket watches—are more than just decoration, so they occasionally find their way in to my wardrobe accessories.

For my taste, any jewelry that performs a function is good to go. And that includes my simple, tasteful, fourteen-karat wedding ring.

It functions as a gift, promise, symbol, and reminder.

Even though we picked them out together, the rings Rita and I exchanged were *gifts*. Me to her. Her to me. If the person with whom you're going to spend the rest of your life gives you a gift, it's wise to accept it graciously and use it for the purpose for which it was intended. That's good advice for just about all the gifts you receive from a loved one.

When we exchanged rings, I made a *promise*. Which brings us to one of those cute stories I don't tell often enough.

Planning our wedding ceremony, Rita and I had talked about

writing our own vows. We decided we would have the pastor lead us through the repeat-after-me stuff—"I, Jay, take you, Rita..." and all that. But while we were slipping rings on each other's left hands, we would share a few words specially prepared for the day. Here's what I said:

> Take this ring as a sign of my love and fidelity. Wear it always to remind you and me of the promise we make today before our family, friends, and most importantly, before God. Our goal is growth. The growth of Rita. The growth of Jay. The growth of Rita and Jay. Together, with God's help, let's remember there's no mountain we can't climb. No river we can't cross. Thanks for marrying me.

Not bad for a twenty-two-year-old punk, right? Well, I slipped that wedding ring on her finger and waited to hear the heartfelt words Rita had composed. It turns out she was a little choked up and forgot what she had written. She paused for a moment, looked at me, and said, "Me too."

Our 250 guests appreciated the humor of the moment, and I guess I did too. Decades later, I stand by my promise. Rita does too.

Of course, a wedding ring is also a *symbol*. If you've been to more than a few weddings, you've heard a preacher talk about how a ring is a never-ending circle symbolizing the eternal promise made by a bride and groom. That works for me. May I add that it's also a practical sign telling the world that I've made a vow that I intend to keep.

Which bring us to the idea of the wedding ring serving as a *reminder*. Here's where you might gain a new perspective on the tradition. You might think that looking at the ring on my finger reminds me to keep my commitment to our vows. But remember, the ring was a gift. Which means it represents her commitment to me! That's something that I can count on and that keeps me coming back for more. In the same way, I'm hoping Rita delights in my commitment to her every time she looks at her ring.

Finally, I'm fully aware that you may not be married or might not have any desire to wear a wedding ring. This chapter—and probably the next—may not apply to you. Hope you understand where I'm coming from.

But I do have to say, my wedding ring is one of my most prized possessions. And I'm more than gratified that it was on God's shopping list for me.

Checking the List

Worth noting. After all this time, I can still slide that ring off my finger and give it a full-minute spin on a flat surface. I just can't do it when Rita's around. She'll inevitably snatch it off the table midspin and maybe even give me the stink eye. Bless her!

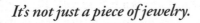 *It's not just a piece of jewelry.*

Wedding Attire

This author cannot and should not address the issue of how much to spend on a wedding dress. It's a special day. One of a kind. And most brides have been imagining the perfect dress since they were little girls. I shudder at some of the outrageous price tags. I also know there are all kinds of slightly unscrupulous purveyors who willingly take advantage of young ladies who are in a vulnerable emotional state as they choose the perfect dress. I recommend walking into any wedding dress emporium with your eyes open accompanied by a levelheaded bridesmaid to whom you've given authority to keep you on budget.

On this topic, I would warn fathers of the bride (or whoever is paying the bill) to make your case for moderation just once, early on, and then let nature take its course. You pretty much need to allow the bride to visit any wedding boutique and try on any dress she wants. In the end, she'll probably stay fairly close to budget. Again, this is a once-in-a-lifetime event.

As for the groom? That's another story. And here's my recommendation. It's a strategy I saw work wonderfully for all four of my sons: Don't make your best man and groomsmen rent tuxedos. The cost is astronomical, the hassle of getting measured and fitted is not worth the effort, and rented tuxes don't fit that well anyway. Plus, no one is looking at you! For good reason, the bride's gown and bridesmaids' dresses get all the visual attention.

Instead, have all the guys wear the same color suit and—as a gift— buy them matching ties.

Think about it. Every young man needs a good dark suit, and being part of a wedding party is a good excuse to make that investment. When you tell your college roommate, your work pal, and your kid brother that they don't have to spring for a $200 tuxedo rental, they'll be thrilled. Then tell them to take that same amount of money and buy a good midrange suit.

This is not a new idea. An internet search will reveal several retail menswear chains that cater to wedding parties. Sure, they rent tuxedos. But they also will help coordinate suit shopping for all the groomsmen, even those who live in other parts of the country. It's not as complicated as it sounds. You may even invite the fathers of the bride and groom to pick up the same style and color of suit. Feel free to go traditional— dark gray or navy—or do your own thing. My son Alec chose seersucker for his summer backyard wedding.

Make sense? I hope so. The only other wedding advice this author has is this. The couple's wedding day is like no other. Everyone involved needs to get on board, keep smiling, and take nothing personally. The decisions about who attends, who stands up, who walks down the aisle, where, when, how, and why are breathtakingly complex. Some decisions were made before the bride and groom ever met, some were made the day of the engagement, and some are made minutes before the ceremony. The way the events of the big weekend unfold are influenced by tradition, budget, religious affiliations, the mother of the bride, and a gazillion other factors that are out of the control of even the happy couple. Don't you dare have any hard feelings based on who sat where, plus ones, travel schedules, wedding photos that take too long, or the lack of gluten-free hors d'oeuvres.

So maybe this chapter is not so much about wedding dresses and tuxedos but more a reminder that doing life together with family and friends creates all kinds of opportunities to give and take. To share wisdom and work together. To consider the needs of others and sometimes let others have their way.

Weddings are a chance to root enthusiastically for the bride and groom while praying that this is the first day of a wonderful blessings-filled life together.

Eloping works too.

Checking the List

Weddings, funerals, anniversary parties, and family reunions can often bring families closer together, providing opportunities to heal old wounds, forget grudges, and acknowledge that disagreements from the past are water under the bridge. But just as likely is that ever-so-brief moment of conflict or miscommunication that regretfully does just the opposite. Do whatever it takes to prevent that from happening or minimize the hurt feelings.

 What you wear isn't nearly as important as who you are.

Juggling Balls

You need to learn to juggle. Really. It's not terribly hard, yet it's still kind of impressive. With just a bit of effort, you might pick it up right away, or it might take a few twenty-minute practice sessions. But even if you're a bit of a klutz, I recommend you give it a try. All by yourself, without an audience. If you fail, no worries.

Colorful juggling balls are readily available online, but really, you don't need to purchase any special equipment. For your first self-taught lesson you can use any three balls, right around the size and weight of a typical baseball. Procure something sphere-ish you can easily toss two feet in the air and catch without thinking about it too hard. Then do that. A hundred times. With one hand, toss up and catch, using only your peripheral vision to secure the catch. Then do it with the other hand. Master that, and you are 90 percent of the way to juggling three baseballs, bean bags, marshmallows, oranges, or juggling balls.

If you were in my front yard with me, I'd demonstrate the next step. But since we're not, I'm going to turn the rest of this lesson over to YouTube. You can find several good instructional videos by searching "learn to juggle." The only insight I can add to what you might learn online is to go ahead and talk to yourself while you are learning.

As you move each ball horizontally across your waist and begin each toss, you might even say, "Swoop. Swoop. Swoop."

Got it? Ready to go for it? Put the book down and give it a try. Good luck!

Now let's move on to the real point of this chapter. *Throwing is more important than catching.* If you attempt to juggle, you will quickly realize that catching is easy…if the toss is done right.

The same is true in real-life conversations and other human interaction. As much as possible, make it easy for others to "catch what you throw." Give them a fighting chance to respond effectively to your requests and invitations. Anytime you give an assignment or expect someone to follow through with a project on your behalf, make sure they have all the information they need and plenty of time. Too often, we assume family and coworkers have the knowledge, experience, and bandwidth to deal efficiently with our requests. We toss them a problem, but it comes too fast, too high, or too slippery.

Examples? We email a giant file of MP3s and get angry when the intended receiver can't open it. We expect our sixteen-year-old with the new driver's license to navigate city traffic. We give a Jewish colleague a project to be completed over Yom Kippur. We schedule a meeting at Starbucks but don't say which one.

Can you see how our toss led to their failure? A little forethought and a little empathy for the catcher—considering their perspective—increase the chance that they can receive and complete our request in a timely manner. Win-win-win.

I hope the metaphor makes sense. A good toss makes for an easy catch. A bad toss creates an emergency that leads to the next toss being terrible and the next catch being impossible.

Checking the List

I taught all five of my kids to juggle in the summer after their sixth grade. Before that, it would have been too frustrating. That skill has not brought them fame or fortune, but it did give them a bit of confidence and bring a smidge of amusement to their lives. At the time, they probably didn't realize they were also learning empathy, project management, emergency avoidance, and how to set up friends and coworkers for success.

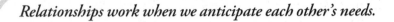 *Relationships work when we anticipate each other's needs.*

Our Daily Bread

Don't ever let someone claim the Bible is out of date and has no application to today's world. It contains more than 2,300 verses on a topic that is top of mind and universally relevant for just about everyone you come across. That topic is money and possessions.

Here are just a few portions of Scripture that contain solid financial wisdom and advice for everyone—even folks who don't believe in God.

- "Whoever loves money never has enough; whoever loves wealth is never satisfied with their income" (Ecclesiastes 5:10).

- "The wicked borrow and do not repay, but the righteous give generously" (Psalm 37:21).

- "Don't begin until you count the cost. For who would begin construction of a building without first calculating the cost to see if there is enough money to finish it?" (Luke 14:28 NLT).

- "Work brings profit, but mere talk leads to poverty!" (Proverbs 14:23 NLT).

- "For the love of money is a root of all kinds of evil. Some people, eager for money, have wandered from the faith and pierced themselves with many griefs" (1 Timothy 6:10).

- "A sluggard's appetite is never filled, but the desires of the diligent are fully satisfied" (Proverbs 13:4).

- "Where your treasure is, there your heart will be also" (Matthew 6:21).

On the topic of money, the Bible is surprising, honest, penetrating, and universally relevant. Guys in every tax bracket have firsthand experience about how money can absolutely control your life. Sometimes destroy it.

The funny thing is that the Bible never says money is bad. Rather, greed is bad. Get-rich-quick schemes are bad. Not paying your debts is bad. Seeing a brother in need and not sharing is bad. But the truth is that money and possessions are not inherently evil. David, Solomon, Job, Abraham, and other biblical heroes were abundantly wealthy. Like the rest of us, they made some bad decisions along the way. But for the most part, they had their act together when it came to money.

So what about today? How can we stop the stranglehold of conspicuous consumption? The assumption that more is better? Obsessing about investments? Comparing our stuff with their stuff? Seeking gratification with online orders delivered next day to my front door? Maxing out our credit cards?

Stopping that enslavement may be a simple three-step process—an awareness, really.

First, recognize the temporal nature of possessions. Earthly stuff doesn't last. "Do not store up for yourselves treasures on earth, where moths and vermin destroy, and where thieves break in and steal" (Matthew 6:19).

Second, realize that everything in the world was created and is still owned by God. Even those things you bought with your own money aren't really yours. They are gifts from a generous Creator God. Who, by the way, also gave you the ability to earn money or make those cherished possessions.

And third, God promises to meet your needs day after day. He provided manna for the Israelites wandering the desert on the way to the Promised Land. He clothes the flowers of the field and feeds the birds of the air. So trust him, and he will care for you. "My God will meet all your needs according to the riches of his glory in Christ Jesus" (Philippians 4:19).

So maybe this chapter is unnecessary. God doesn't want you to put this item on your personal shopping list. He's already promising to provide it. But it would be a good idea for you to keep praying with heartfelt gratitude, "Give us this day our daily bread."

Checking the List

If you accept God as your heavenly Father, this all makes sense. Matthew 7:9-11 approaches God's provision logically: "Which of you, if your son asks for bread, will give him a stone? Or if he asks for a fish, will give him a snake? If you, then, though you are evil, know how to give good gifts to your children, how much more will your Father in heaven give good gifts to those who ask him!"

 Trust in God's ultimate, timely, and complete provision.

Peeps, Candy Corn, Peanut Brittle, Pumpkin-Spice Lattes, Shamrock Shakes, and So On

You very likely know someone who goes a little bonkers for a specific seasonal sweet treat. The object of their affection is a mostly affordable packaged good or specialty item that becomes available at certain times of the year in drug stores or fast-food restaurants across the country.

The annual craving by your friend or loved one is not an obsession or addiction. It's not illegal or dangerous. Although you certainly wouldn't call it healthy, you would probably admit there's something life giving about it. Something beautifully uplifting, really. And it's something that God just might have for your shopping list.

The best example of this annual opportunity might be my bride Rita's appreciation for the Peeps deliveries to our home in the weeks leading up to Easter.

They arrive via courier, US Postal Service, hand delivery, or in unmarked packages left on our front porch. I must say, just the presence of those frighteningly addictive marshmallow-covered-with-flavored-sugar bunnies and chicks brings an outpouring of joy and appreciation. You see, my wife loves Peeps. But more than that, she loves being remembered. (Don't we all?)

It's become an annual contest. The first person in the family who notices that Peeps have arrived in the local drugstore will inevitably start the Peeps parade. One recent spring, my sons Alec and Max showed up with at least six packages of Peeps. One of every color available.

As an aside, please note that I never purchase Peeps. I don't have to. Which is fine with me, because frankly, I don't even like Peeps. I do, however, like the tradition. It's an undeniable source of happiness in our family—for both the receiver and the givers. I couldn't stop it even if I tried.

So what's the preferred holiday treat for someone you care about? That friend, coworker, family member, or neighbor. Is it pumpkin-spice donuts or candy corn in October? Is it candy canes, fruitcake, or peanut brittle in December? Maybe you need to buy an extra box of Thin Mints or Do-si-dos from the Girl Scouts each year. Not for yourself, but for that one person whose eyes light up when they see those classic recognizable cookie boxes.

The gift may be delicious. But the real gift is that you remembered. You were thinking about that person. You went out of your way to stop by that store, place that order, or drive through that fast food joint and then make the delivery.

Really, the best part about this item on your shopping list is that you don't have to write it down or remember it. All you have to do is go about your business. The retailer, restaurant, or fundraiser will remind you. When Shamrock Shakes come out at McDonald's, pick up a couple medium-size shakes, drive to the home of your old friend, and toast Saint Patrick's Day. When Dunkin' starts advertising pumpkin-spice lattes, invite your mom, sister, or aunt out for coffee. When Peeps hit the store shelves, send a box to my wife.

You get the idea. We're really talking about recalling and acting. How often do we have fond recollections about someone but fail to act?

- *My old neighbor, Mrs. Feldman, used to make the best fruitcake.*

- *Candy corn? My brother Marty is the only person I know who likes it.*

- *Every year, Aunt Polly would buy four boxes of Thin Mints from me.*

In the next year, if some commercial on the radio or trip down a seasonal aisle triggers a thought like this, you know what to do. Buy a fruitcake, bag of candy corn, or box of Thin Mints, and make that delivery.

Checking the List

In 1 Corinthians 11:2, we read, "I praise you for remembering me in everything and for holding to the traditions just as I passed them on to you." Of course, the apostle Paul is commending the church at Corinth for remembering his prior teachings and honoring traditions of the early church. He's confirming that intentional interactions and commemorations are the foundation for discipleship. Building relationships and putting others ahead of ourselves will make our lives and our faith attractive to others, especially those with whom we have a history of friendship and family.

 Small gestures lead to significant bonds.

Small Group That Actually Holds You Accountable

If you're in a small group, I invite you to imagine this scenario. During the time set aside for prayer requests, you courageously reveal a secret personal burden you'd like to eliminate. God has been convicting you in a certain area of your life, and you realize it's time to bring it up to this trusted group of friends who will surely have some godly insight and provide steps to put this bad habit, possible addiction, or sinful pattern behind you.

You've searched Scripture and found verses like James 5:16, "Confess your sins to each other and pray for each other so that you may be healed," and Proverbs 27:17, "As iron sharpens iron, so one person sharpens another."

You're counting on this circle of friends to hear you, sharpen you, and pray for you because you're feeling broken by sin and have a sincere desire to be healed.

What might you be confessing? It could be anything. You spend too much time on social media. You spend too much money on shoes. A few times a week, you find yourself clicking over to unseemly websites. A few times a day, you feel yourself getting angry at your toddler or teenager for almost no reason at all. You know your home is the right size, but reality television has you mildly obsessing over a place that's bigger and better. You gossip, hold grudges, or flirt with your married neighbor.

So after praying and considering all the repercussions, you open your heart and spill your guts. In that scenario, how does your trusted small group respond? Mind you, your sin is not brazen or scandalous. A little envy, a little lust, a little anger…what's the big deal? No one is getting hurt. No one is going to jail.

Again, how do they respond? In way too many small groups, your peers do the unthinkable. They let you off the hook.

It's close to tragic, but just about every member of your so-called accountability group says, "I have the same problem" or "Don't be so hard on yourself" or some such thing. It's almost as if the other members of the group are thinking, *My baggage is so much worse, I need to downplay any shame or judgment so I can feel less guilty about my own sins.*

When that happens, your small group, Bible study, life group, or missional community that is specifically designed to create disciples and help each other live in obedience to God's Word has failed.

How should they respond? They should be listening with empathy, asking penetrating questions, getting to the heart of those sins you're confessing, encouraging you to take ownership of those sins, grieving, admonishing, and helping you identify strategies that move you away from lifestyle choices and patterns that lead to that sin. Yes, they can still be encouragers—even cheerleaders—but initially they need to deliver truth and offer biblical guidance.

It's not easy. For you or them. You're asking a lot from a group of men or women, most of whom have not been to seminary or Bible college. But isn't that the point of a small group? With love and grace, holding each other to the highest possible standards.

So how about your small group? When a member bares his or her soul, is there a flurry of rationalizing, excuse making, or minimizing the problem? Might the group collectively laugh it off with a joke or two? Does the confessor start to play the victim, blaming the circumstance or blaming Satan? Is there a halfhearted confession without a change in behavior?

Here's a common response that on the surface might seem like a good strategy. Someone in the group says, "Let's pray for you." *But it's too soon.* Surely, prayer invites God's intervention, but that's only part of the solution. The problem should first be fully identified or confessed. Look again at James 5:16 and note the need for both confession and prayer: "Confess your sins to each other and pray for each other so that you may be healed."

By far, the most likely response is just letting it slide. The member gives a partial confession, and the group is way too eager to let the guilty party off the hook.

Well, if that's what happens at your small group or Bible study, you have two options. Put "new small group" on your shopping list. Or take it upon yourself—along with your current group leader—to provoke change. Be proactive. Don't wait until your group experiences the scenario described in this chapter.

Last thought. If this chapter doesn't apply because you're not in an accountability group of some kind, then you definitely have a worthwhile new item for your shopping list.

Checking the List

We can't leave this idea of meeting regularly with a vibrant small group without quoting the classic verse from Hebrews 10:24-25: "Let us consider how we may spur one another on toward love and good deeds, not giving up meeting together, as some are in the habit of doing, but encouraging one another—and all the more as you see the Day approaching."

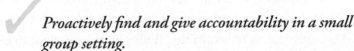 *Proactively find and give accountability in a small group setting.*

The Right Tool for the Right Job

B e honest—have you ever used a flat-edge screwdriver or a wood chisel to open a can of paint? Tsk-tsk.

How about standing tiptoe on a kitchen chair—and almost killing yourself—to reach a lightbulb just because you were too lazy to go out to the garage to get the stepladder? You know better than that!

Or maybe you recently attempted to create a spreadsheet with word processing software because you had not yet learned how to use Excel or Google Sheets. Ask anyone who works in an office—it's worth taking the time to learn your way around the most popular office software.

In other words, it's important to acquire and master the right tools for whatever job God puts in front of you.

To be clear, you don't have to own every tool, apparatus, utensil, or weapon that's ever been invented. Only if you're hunting whales do you need a harpoon. Only if you're delivering blocks of ice in the early twentieth century would you need giant ice tongs. Only kayakers need kayak paddles. Only catchers need a catcher's mask. The tools you need are the ones you're going to actually use.

In the same conversation is this idea: Just because you've had success with a tool doesn't mean it's the right tool to use for every situation. Said another way is the warning "If all you have is a hammer, every problem will look like a nail."

As a radio producer, I experienced that firsthand. Earlier in my career in Christian media, I successfully launched short radio features for several ministries, including the National Center for Fathering, Voice of the Martyrs, the Heritage Foundation, and the Bible League. Because they were public service announcements, my nonprofit clients didn't have to pay for any airtime. My fees were modest. Hundreds of stations across the country faithfully aired these little PSAs, some for more than twenty years. We reached literally millions of listeners with valuable information and encouragement, and the ministries were delighted.

With that modest track record, I erroneously assumed I had stumbled on a media formula that would work for every ministry with any message for all audiences.

As a result—for a few years—the only "tool" I ever recommended for a new client was for them to launch a short daily radio PSA. For several clients who followed my recommendation, the results were less than impressive. For those clients, I hang on to a bit of regret. At least I was smart enough to recommend they pull the plug after the first six months or so.

All that to say, know your tools—know how, when, and why they are most effective—and use them wisely. And add the right tools at the right time.

So what tools might you need to add to your toolbox? The possibilities are endless. Should you learn a foreign language, join Toastmasters, or get an MBA or ministry certification? Maybe it's time to learn a trade, anything from welding to masonry to aviation maintenance.

As you enter the next season of life—graduation, living on your own, marriage, home ownership, parenting, serving in ministry, seeking full-time employment—what talents do you need to sharpen, or what skill do you need to learn?

Evaluating your tools is something you should be doing regularly. Or you may want to take advantage of a professional career and skills assessment service. Choose a program that keeps up with changing technology and workplace environments and uses a variety of assessment tools, including aptitude tests, interviews, and cognitive exploration.

The takeaway for this chapter might be this: On God's shopping list is for you to take full advantage of the many tools on which your name has already been engraved. Some you already own and have mastered. Some are waiting unused on your workbench. Some are yet undiscovered. Those hidden gifts will be fully revealed only after you've committed yourself to a long-term vision, failed more than once, learned from your mistakes, set aside your fears, and reached out of your comfort zone to best fulfill the plan God has just for you.

Checking the List

Mastering all the tools God has supplied on your workbench won't necessarily lead to a new career or direction for your life. On the other hand, digging deep and really uncovering how your mind, body, and spirit work together might lead to great wealth and fame. Or it could be simply making you a better parent, friend, employee, or neighbor. Remember, it's not about you.

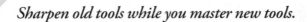 *Sharpen old tools while you master new tools.*

Little Things

C all me old-fashioned, but I still think a woman's purse should contain a short list of items that may come in handy to meet her own needs or the needs of those in her immediate acquaintance. Items to consider include lip balm, hand sanitizer, rubber bands, nail clippers, matches, breath mints, discreetly wrapped feminine hygiene items, makeup essentials, pepper spray, lens wipes, a small sewing kit, Band-Aids, tissues, something to write with, something to write on, and something to help a headache.

You'll note these are not expensive items. Including them on God's shopping list is not a major financial decision. Also, I fully realize women's purses come in at least three sizes—the beach purse, the everyday purse, and the date purse. Because of the diminutive size of a date purse, feel free to forego most of these items (except the breath mints).

As for the gentlemen? If you carry a backpack, messenger bag, or man-bag, then all the above apply. In addition, I have long believed that every man should always have in his possession a clean handkerchief. Possibly monogrammed. Probably white, but not necessarily. In some parts of the country, a bandana would suffice.

Hankies are wonderfully handy for a myriad of manly reasons. As a tourniquet to stop severe bleeding. To clean spectacles. To dry your hands when today's loud air-blowing hand dryers fail. To mop your brow after performing manly duties out in the sun. To blow your nose. And if absolutely necessary, to signal surrender to an enemy.

Perhaps most importantly, you never know when a gentleman might be called upon to offer his neatly folded handkerchief to a lady who may be tearing up because that's what ladies do when they are extremely happy or extremely sad.

Little things matter more than you may realize. That becomes apparent during a minor emergency when a small inexpensive item is desperately needed but not available. Mechanics, lawyers, architects, chefs, and many other technicians or professionals will confirm that truth. All the time and money spent on big things quickly become secondary to that little necessity you don't have.

So don't miss the small things on God's shopping list.

Actually, small stuff may be the most important stuff of all. As Dante said, "A mighty flame followeth a tiny spark." And Ben Franklin said, "A small leak can sink a great ship."

The Bible confirms that God delights in using small things and that they should never be taken for granted. Consider the small beginnings of a mustard plant: "Though it is the smallest of all seeds, yet when it grows, it is the largest of garden plants and becomes a tree, so that the birds come and perch in its branches" (Matthew 13:32).

Then there's the widow who offered her last two copper coins for the temple collection box. "'Truly I tell you,' [Jesus] said, 'this poor widow has put in more than all the others. All these people gave their gifts out of their wealth; but she out of her poverty put in all she had to live on'" (Luke 21:3-4).

Consider John 6, where Jesus used five barley loaves and two small fish from the basket of a small boy to feed thousands.

Coming full circle, what are you carrying in your pocket or purse? An argument can be made regarding the benefits of traveling light. It's true, God will provide everything you need. But did you consider that sometimes you are the person he might use to provide for someone else? Your Band-Aid, handkerchief, or sewing kit might save the day for a colleague or stranger. Your gift of a copper penny or loaf of bread could mean the difference between life or death—or make an eternal difference—for someone you may never meet.

God has major plans for your future. So think big. In the meantime, the most important thing for you to do is take care of the details. In the parable of the shrewd manager, Jesus confirms, "Whoever can be trusted with very little can also be trusted with much" (Luke 16:10).

Checking the List

Perhaps do an inventory of your bags and pockets. Do the contents represent who God wants you to be? What should you rid yourself of? What should you be carrying, just in case?

 Is what you are carrying a benefit or a burden?

Mustard

The reason God might put mustard on your shopping list is because he wants you to stand in front of the mustard shelf at your local supermarket and consider the options.

I did that last week at my local Jewel store. Guess how many choices I had? Seventy-seven. In the condiment aisle were fifty-six different styles and sizes, including Grey Poupon, French's Classic Yellow Mustard, and something called Inglehoffer Original Stone Ground Mustard. Over in the deli section, I found fourteen more spreadable and squeezable options. And in the spice aisle, there were seven varieties of mustard spice and seeds. In other corners of the store, I also came across mustard greens, sweet mustard barbecue sauce, two different bags of honey mustard pretzels, three different options for mustard potato salad, and three styles of canned sardines in Dijon mustard. But let's not count those.

Some of my books get translated into foreign languages and have been distributed in fascinating and divergent parts of the world. If you happen to be reading this in Swahili, Yoruba, Zulu, or any other sub-Saharan language of Africa, I apologize. I'm not even sure if you care for mustard, but I am reasonably sure you can't walk into anything resembling an American supermarket and have those kinds of choices. I am also sure I don't know enough about your culture to know whether that matters to you. You may be wonderfully content with the food, spices, and sauces you have available. I hope so.

To be clear, this chapter is not about hunger. Children and families on every continent—and perhaps in every country—regularly go to bed hungry. Just that thought should break our hearts. To help remedy that tragic situation, may I recommend you respond with prayer and generosity, volunteering and financially supporting relief efforts as the Lord leads?

Instead, this chapter is about being distracted by choices. Not the critical choices between good and evil—those need your full attention. We're talking about making choices that keep us from spending time with Jesus or divert our attention from our role as kingdom builders. Two examples from Scripture come to mind.

Luke 10 describes the evening that Martha invited Jesus into her home. It turns out that Martha's sister, Mary, didn't let house cleaning or meal preparation distract her from literally sitting at the feet of Jesus. As Jesus clearly states, she made the better choice.

> [Martha] had a sister called Mary, who sat at the Lord's feet listening to what he said. But Martha was distracted by all the preparations that had to be made. She came to him and asked, "Lord, don't you care that my sister has left me to do the work by myself? Tell her to help me!"
>
> "Martha, Martha," the Lord answered, "you are worried and upset about many things, but few things are needed— or indeed only one. Mary has chosen what is better, and it will not be taken away from her" (Luke 10:39-42).

In the Sermon on the Mount, Jesus tells his disciples not to worry about food, drink, or clothes. Reading that admonishment, most people immediately think Jesus is talking about the fear of not having enough to eat, drink, or wear. In context, that's probably an accurate evaluation of the main point of this passage. But in modern America, don't we spend a whole lot of energy deciding where to eat and go for coffee? And how much time do you stand in front of your closet asking yourself, *What am I going to wear?*

With that perspective, take a fresh read of Matthew 6:31-33:

> So don't ever worry by saying, "What are we going to eat?" or "What are we going to drink?" or "What are we going to wear?" because it is the unbelievers who are eager for all those things. Surely your heavenly Father knows that you need all of them! But first be concerned about God's kingdom and his righteousness, and all of these things will be provided for you as well (ISV).

With these two passages in mind, here's a request for the next time you find yourself passing a fully stocked shelf of mustard in your favorite supermarket. Remember this chapter and let these two prayerful thoughts go through your head:

- *Thank you, God, for the abundance of your provision.*
- *Please don't let the many choices I have to make distract me from pursuing your kingdom and your righteousness.*

Checking the List

Choice is not a bad thing. The diversity of creation invites us to choose between a variety of species, colors, emotions, weather patterns, ecosystems, experiences, and personalities. It's all God's gift to humanity. But the choices we make reflect the way we see God at work in our lives. So don't be distracted by decisions. Instead, be intentional about choosing God's best.

 Choose faith, hope, and love.

Telescope

O r tickets to an observatory that gives a sense of the size and scope of the universe. Or maybe a chart of the constellations. Or perhaps coolest of all, an app for your smartphone or iPad that allows you to point your device toward the night sky and uses augmented reality to help you identify stars and constellations. Apps that are currently free include Star Chart, Night Sky Lite, GoSkyWatch Planetarium, or Sky View Free. NASA offers a version that includes the latest missions, tracks satellites, and live streams NASA TV.

The reason God might have a stargazing item on your shopping list is threefold. First, to make sure you remain humble. It's a big universe, and we are minor specks. That makes the fact that God loves each one of us even more amazing.

Second, so we can better understand and appreciate significant portions of Scripture. For example, the true story of creation.

> And God said, "Let there be lights in the expanse of the heavens to separate the day from the night. And let them be for signs and for seasons, and for days and years, and let them be lights in the expanse of the heavens to give light upon the earth." And it was so. And God made the two great lights—the greater light to rule the day and the lesser

light to rule the night—and the stars. And God set them in the expanse of the heavens to give light on the earth, to rule over the day and over the night, and to separate the light from the darkness. And God saw that it was good (Genesis 1:14-18 ESV).

Contemplating the night sky also reinforces the promise to Abram that he would have countless descendants. That promise came directly from God. No angel. No scroll. No question about it, and it helped keep Abraham on task while he founded the Jewish nation.

Then the LORD took Abram outside and said to him, "Look up into the sky and count the stars if you can. That's how many descendants you will have!" (Genesis 15:5 NLT).

At first, Abram laughed at the idea. After all, he was 100, and his wife was 90. Later, he totally misinterpreted God's plan, took matters in his own hands, and fathered a son with his wife's maidservant. But God kept his promise, even changing Abram's name to Abraham, which means father of many. Sarah gave birth to Isaac, who would be the first in a long line of descendants that would include the Messiah— the one whose birth was welcomed by the "star of wonder" that guided the wise men of the East to the Christ child.

Third, an appreciation for the sweep of stars above gives us a sense of God's majesty and our purpose. More than a dozen psalms mention stars, the heavens, the night sky, and a light in the darkness. Not to be missed is Psalm 8, which explains that our place in the universe is no accident.

When I consider your heavens,
    the work of your fingers,
the moon and the stars,
    which you have set in place,
what is mankind that you are mindful of them,
    human beings that you care for them?

You have made them a little lower than the angels
  and crowned them with glory and honor.
You made them rulers over the works of your hands;
  you put everything under their feet:
all flocks and herds,
  and the animals of the wild,
the birds in the sky,
  and the fish in the sea,
  all that swim the paths of the seas.

LORD, our Lord,
  how majestic is your name in all the earth! (Psalm
  8:3-9).

When we look at the constellations filling the night sky, we get just a glimpse of the glory of God and find clear confirmation that he cares for us. The stars are one more gift to us from a generous, unfathomable, living God.

Checking the List

Abraham never did count all the stars. That would be impossible. But he did put his complete trust in God, who put the stars in place. And so can we.

 See God's glory. See your place in the universe.

Fire Insurance

Umm...stick with me here because while this chapter title is a pun, it's not at all a laughing matter.

Hell is a real place, described in Revelation 21:8 as a "fiery lake of burning sulfur." I am not sure if that is a literal description of hell or a metaphor, but I suggest you don't take any chances. Whether there are actual flames or not, you most definitely don't want to spend eternity there. Especially when you have the option of living in a mansion in heaven prepared for you by Jesus himself. Eternity is a long time. And the promise of heaven is only moments away if you take the time to really understand what Jesus did on the cross, truly believe it, and choose to receive the free gift of grace.

How do I get that fire insurance policy? you may wonder. Read these six verses a couple times. Consider what they're saying and then take them to heart.

- "All have sinned and fall short of the glory of God" (Romans 3:23).

- "The wages of sin is death, but the gift of God is eternal life in Christ Jesus our Lord" (Romans 6:23).

- "God so loved the world that he gave his one and only Son, that whoever believes in him shall not perish but have eternal life" (John 3:16).

- "If we confess our sins, he is faithful and just and will forgive us our sins and purify us from all unrighteousness" (1 John 1:9).

- "It is by grace you have been saved, through faith—and this is not from yourselves, it is the gift of God" (Ephesians 2:8).

- "God will raise us from the dead by his power, just as he raised our Lord from the dead" (1 Corinthians 6:14 NLT).

Did you get it? We all have sinned. Sin leaves us spiritually dead, separated from God. But God's love and mercy provide a way out. Jesus paid the penalty for our sins on the cross. It's a free gift. Our responsibility is to believe and bring this request before God the Father, and—empowered by the Holy Spirit—we can partner in the resurrection of Christ Jesus.

Make sense? I hope so. If you can turn this idea into the prayer of your heart, I would like to be the first to welcome you into the family as a child of God.

My recommendation is to tell someone you trust about the decision you made and the prayer you prayed. Then put this book down and go read one of the Gospels—probably Matthew or John—so you can really get to know Jesus through his words and actions.

Again, congratulations. If you are so inclined, track me down at jaypayleitner.com and let me know. What a blast it would be to hear from you.

Checking the List

Not everyone who picks up a book like this is an authentic follower of

Christ. If you're just exploring your options, this might be just the right date and time to choose eternal life. Your life will never be the same.

 Maybe think of it not as fire insurance but as a ticket to glory.

Sock Rings

Here halfway through this book on discerning what might be on God's shopping list, I need to confirm what you already know. Many of these items are not items. They are ideas or attitudes we need to pursue. Character traits like ambition. Frugality. Creative vision. A heart for outreach. Time with our families. Realigned priorities. Pursuing these concepts may or may not cost money, but they will require an intentional investment of time, determination, commitment, and effort. If you've read this far, you get the idea.

But this chapter is about something you can and should actually buy—if you wear socks. And especially if you have multiple sock wearers in the house.

I'm talking about sock rings. If you don't know what they are, Google it. There are different styles and brands. They're also known as sock sorters, sock clips, and sock holders. They have brand names like SockLocks and EX Pro Sock Holders.

Rita and I have raised five kids—four sons and a daughter. All athletes who quite often wore multiple pairs of socks each day. My children were not allowed to put socks in the laundry unless they were matched and secured with sock rings. We did not have a zillion house rules, but that was one of them. Over the years, that rule may have saved us hundreds of dollars and hundreds of hours matching socks. And also saved the Payleitner men from the great humiliation of leaving the house with two different socks. (Although I think Isaac did that anyway.)

Faithful use of sock rings also saves you from the aggravating frustration of holding in your hand one sock from a favorite pair and knowing its mate is gone forever. It's happened to all of us. And you just want to scream "Nooooooo!" Even more frustrating is holding on to that lone sock with the hope that the companion sock eventually surfaces, while deep down you know it never will.

Or even worse, you finally throw out the lone sock, and a week later the matching sock crawls out from under your bed.

One last thought about lost socks. There are several theories out there regarding where lost socks go and what happens to them. One theory is that sock manufacturers are in collusion with dryer manufacturers, and dryers are designed to eat the occasional sock during the tumble-dry cycle. Another theory is that socks are the pupae stage of adult wire hangers. That's why every time you can't find a sock, you do find another wire hanger in the bottom of your closet. Sock rings rescue you from both those scenarios and any other mystical force that dispatches perfectly good socks into a third dimension, twilight zone, or secret holding cell.

I *believe* in sock rings. I've thought about *selling* sock rings. But instead, I share it with you with no profit motive.

So if you have a house filled with young athletes who wear three pairs of socks every day—or even if it's just you—consider going online and ordering several packs of sock rings.

Checking the List

When you find something that works—whether it's something to make life easier or something that helps you gain an eternal perspective—it's natural to share it with the world.

 Enjoy using any device that saves time, money, and frustration!

Anything in the Shopping Cart

It was a Sunday afternoon a few years ago. An impromptu, serendipitous gathering of my five adult children plus three daughters-in-law. With no specific plans.

And of course, we were all hungry.

If it had been a holiday, Rita and I—well in advance—would have worked out a strategy for feeding this worthy crew made up of our favorite people in the world. We would have planned some combination of appetizers, roasted turkey, pans of lasagna, pork chops on the grill, Italian beef, homemade or takeout pizza, plus an array of veggie trays, cut-up fruit, and a classic dessert. Every family has their favorite go-to recipes and dining traditions.

But again, this was a last-minute, unexpected surprise.

Of course, we could have gone to a local restaurant and spent a couple hours and a couple hundred dollars. But I had a riskier idea.

The ten of us jumped in two cars and drove to Blue Goose Market. Blue Goose is one of those smaller, family-owned grocery stores that is a favorite of the locals. It's a little fresher and a little pricier with a great deli and friendly cashiers. Not unlike a Trader Joe's. The aisles are manageable, and you really can't get lost.

After my brief instructions, we swarmed the aisles and came away with about $117 of food. (Plus a sock monkey.)

The goal was to fill our bellies. The only rule was that anyone could put anything in the cart and—without judgment—it would go through the checkout line. (Including sock monkeys.)

The final menu: Steaks. Cannoli. Tiramisu. Carrot cake mix. Frosting. Salad fixin's. Chips. Lemonade. Raspberry lemonade. Macaroni salad. Sour patch straws. Guacamole. Homemade salsa. Bottled cherry soda. Awesome bread. Slider buns. Horseradish. All in all, a tasty spread. (Except for the sock monkey.)

Back home, the crowded prep kitchen added to the spontaneity of the day. The rib eyes were grilled to perfection. The meal was surprisingly balanced. And everyone cleaned up! Plus, as noted, the final cost was less than taking the crew to most restaurants.

Next time you find yourself with a group of hungry friends or family members and a little bit of time, I recommend you try it. That day, I happened to cover the cost at the checkout, but you could certainly split the cost between participants.

Why might "anything in the shopping cart" be on God's shopping list? That's obvious. The ritual of shopping, meal preparation, and breaking bread is all about celebration, family, and friendship. Done as a group activity, the event embodies creativity, trust, cooperation, and teamwork.

To be honest, the unscripted spontaneous event was simply great fun. When something brings that much joy, I can't help but see God at work.

In Ecclesiastes, Solomon explores the themes of the fleeting nature of life, the uncertainties of the future, and the certainty of death. To combat materialism and bring meaning to our existence, he suggests we find joy in the moment, particularly when we gather over food and drink. Ecclesiastes 9:7 (NLT) reads, "So go ahead. Eat your food with joy, and drink your wine with a happy heart, for God approves of this!"

That Sunday afternoon, I don't recall if any of my kids or their spouses came with a specific burden or a heavy heart. But I know we all left with an elevated spirit and greater appreciation for our lives and each other.

Checking the List

God doesn't want us to be miserable. Yes, there will be challenges in life. Even seasons of sadness. But in general, those who believe in God and have hope for a future in blessed eternity should make it a point to gather in celebration of our joy in knowing Christ.

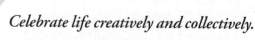 *Celebrate life creatively and collectively.*

Clunkers

I've owned a few…

A '66 Volkswagen Beetle. My senior year of high school, I rolled it attempting to maneuver an icy on-ramp to the Eisenhower Expressway during my early morning delivery job.

A '64 Chevy Biscayne. A gift from my older sister. It didn't survive the Thanksgiving snowstorm of 1978.

A '66 AMC Rambler. Inherited from my late grandfather, who spent forty years as a shift manager at the AMC factory in Kenosha, Wisconsin, where it was built. I'm not sure what ever happened to it.

A '69 Ford Econoline. A former delivery service van, bought for $450. Sold to a swimming pool maintenance service that trashed it less than a year later.

A '77 Toyota Corolla hatchback. Our honeymoon car and our main transportation for at least four years.

The stories these cars could tell. An accident here and there. Road trips to New Orleans and Canada. Several traffic stops but just a couple traffic tickets. Lots of oil changes and driveway maintenance. Embarrassing rust spots. Do-it-yourself paint jobs—one using orange Rust-Oleum and a paint brush. Scraping windows on cold mornings. Sputtering radiators on hot turnpikes.

The best and most frightening story stars the Ford Econoline van. Just a couple months before we were married, Rita and her two sisters used that van to visit their grandmother and pick up an overstuffed armchair. On the way home, Rita drove, Jeanne sat in the passenger seat, and Michelle literally sat in the armchair in the far back.

Waiting to turn left at a red light, Rita looked up to see a rock as big as a cantaloupe bounce out from between the rear tires of a gravel truck and head straight for her face. Her reaction to tip her head slightly to the right saved her life. The rock smashed through the windshield, skimmed Rita's shoulder, flew through the van, broke the top left corner of the overstuffed chair, ricocheted up, dented the ceiling of the van, and landed in Michelle's lap. Seriously.

The truck driver continued without a clue. One witness raced to the driver's side window, expecting the worst. The shattered glass left dozens of tiny cuts on Rita's face and several ounces of glass splinters inside her shirt. Michelle sat stunned in the broken chair. Jeanne looked up from her book and asked, "What was that?" After a few minutes composing herself, Rita drove the van the few miles home with Jeanne holding a pillow over the eight-inch hole in the glass.

In the end, there was no permanent damage except to the chair and the windshield. The chair was tossed. The glass was replaced. We sold the van a few months later. We still have the rock. It's on our fireplace.

Since the Toyota hatchback, we've been able to afford new or almost new vehicles. Including four minivans for our growing family. Those newer cars started every morning, and we felt safe riding with our kids during our daily carpooling and vacation getaways.

So why might clunkers be on God's shopping list? A few reasons.

Certainly, after enduring some frustrations with our high-mileage vehicles, we have a real appreciation for the way God has provided our family with newer cars. Does God really care about our transportation needs? I think he does. He cherishes life and has specific plans for each of us. He provides resources so we can give back to him and give him glory. Driving a few clunkers in my younger days kept me humble, hungry, motivated, vigilant, and frugal. Not bad lessons to learn.

On the topic of car buying. Financial experts suggest that it's wise to pay cash for a vehicle with low miles. There's some truth to the platitude that a new car loses significant value as soon as it's driven off the lot. Saving up for a car also develops self-discipline and avoids the expense of paying interest on your car loan.

In the same vein, I understand why parents might buy their high school sophomore a new car. It's safer and more reliable. But I'm pretty sure that young man or woman will never appreciate the new car smell of their own first new car purchase as much as someone who has suffered through years of driving clunkers, junkers, bombs, jalopies, heaps, or buckets of bolts.

Checking the List

If you're driving a new Lexus or Land Rover, more power to you. As long as you acknowledge that God's provision put it in your driveway. Still, on the road, make sure you have a healthy respect and even a measure of love for those who might be driving with a broken mirror, dented bumper, or some duct tape securing their trunk.

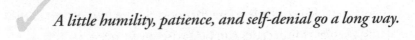 *A little humility, patience, and self-denial go a long way.*

Other Second-String Stuff

In addition to the car you drive, some other items might deserve consideration when choosing second rate, secondhand, or second best. Specifically, that would be possessions that typically have a higher cost or represent a look-at-me status.

You probably shouldn't use price to determine who's performing your appendectomy, dental implants, or LASIK eye surgery. Someone once said, "Don't buy a cheap mattress or cheap shoes. Because if you're not in one, you're probably in the other."

I also don't believe God wants you buying poorly made, cheap carpentry tools, office furniture, kitchen appliances, and other stuff you use every day. Paying a little more for tools that make you more efficient and that last for decades can be a wise investment.

But what about items you might acquire not as an investment but as a status symbol? The vacation home you never have time for. That giant TV that's too big for the room anyway. The motorcycle your spouse doesn't want you to ride. The sailboat or speedboat you constantly compare with all the other boats in the marina. The custom-tailored wardrobe, the conspicuous watch, or the latest must-have tech gadget.

Here are just a few reasons to rethink that purchase.

First, the extra expense. Even if you can afford the payments, that money might be better spent elsewhere. Very few luxury items are investments. If you really do need that just-released XP-Ace-Pro blah-blah-blah 10GHz laptop to maximize your efficiency at work, then go for it. But if it's for show (or for gaming), take a step back.

Second, the added worry. How will you react about the first dent in your new Ferrari? What about the spot of truffles or caviar on your Gucci blazer? (Why are you eating fungi and fish eggs anyway?) Also, the bigger your vacation home, the more time you'll spend monitoring the security system. And how can you enjoy your workout when you spend the entire time worrying about whether your Rolex is safe in your health club locker?

Third, the maintenance. You know the definition of "pleasure boat"? A hole in the water into which you pour money. Also, I don't know this firsthand, but I understand high-end cars require significantly more TLC. Besides, you can't drive it unless the weather is perfect. And if you don't drive it, then what's the point?

Fourth, your priorities. Yes, you love your family and friends. But if you're not careful, you might start caring more about your Harley than your honey. Or the big screen in your family room than your family. Or your status and social ranking than your personal relationships.

Fifth, your spiritual perspective. Stuff distracts. Stuff wears out. Stuff goes out of style. Life is not made of stuff. "[Jesus] said to them, 'Watch out! Be on your guard against all kinds of greed; life does not consist in an abundance of possessions'" (Luke 12:15).

Sixth, chasing the wind. If your identity is wrapped up in possessions, then your value is limited to today. Next time you hear the fanfare for the latest shiny new object, please leave your credit card in your wallet. Don't spend another minute or nickel grasping for the attention of the popular crowd. God sees you as more than your possessions. Besides, what God has prepared for you is bigger and better than anything you could imagine yourself.

Checking the List

Your shopping list should include stuff that lasts. A car that's paid for and starts in the morning. A modest wardrobe in style for more than one season. Well-made tools you can pass on to the next generation. And sure, put vacations on your list. But make sure they are really vacations, not days of stressing over possessions that own you.

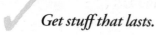 *Get stuff that lasts.*

Question Cards

Have you ever hosted a large gathering of friends or family and the conversation was limited to completely inconsequential chitchat?

Sometimes that's okay. If your brain has been working overtime, you may need to blow off a few hours talking about the ups and downs of the local sports franchise, the new wool yarn at the local knitting store, or the plot of the latest binge-watched cable program. Afterward, you realize that you learned nothing new about your guests and they learned nothing about you. There was nothing even close to a vibrant, healthy exchange of ideas and experiences.

Again, that's not always terrible. There's a place for small talk. But what if you could use a simple tool to turn the conversation up a notch? To really get your family or friends thinking, laughing, sharing, reflecting, and even engaging in a little healthy and respectful debate. Might that kind of resource be on God's shopping list before your next gathering?

Do an online search for "question cards." You'll instantly see several products you can purchase or download to turn your next gathering into a montage of straightforward or deeply thought-provoking questions followed by an array of answers you couldn't possibly expect.

Brand names include Chat Pack, Table Topics, Big Talk, Empowering Questions, and 100 Questions. There's some risk in following the current trend in party and card games, so you'll want to shop wisely and consider your guest list. As I have done, you may want to review and cull the cards to choose the most appropriate questions. If you're ambitious, feel free to make up your own questions.

For years, the Payleitner family has intentionally held off Thanksgiving dessert for an hour or so while we pass around a book or basket of questions. Everyone gets a turn, and you never know what question you're going to get. Over the years, we've heard some surprising responses to simple questions.

"What's your earliest memory?" This led my grandmother, who was born in 1900, to recall the sunny afternoon she was hanging laundry as a young teenager and was amazed when an airplane flew overhead. She had heard about those flying contraptions but had never seen one before.

"What do you want to be doing ten years from now?" One of my children revealed some substantial life plans that no one at the table had ever heard before. It was a memorable moment.

"What's the scariest thing that ever happened to you?" My mom revealed the story from 1944 when she broke off her engagement with a guy who didn't take the news very well. He threatened and stalked her for several days until her brothers stepped in. Her story was gripping. She would meet my father a year later.

Using these card decks is not a high-pressure situation. If someone pulls out a question they don't want to answer, that's fine. Just have them grab another. The host may want to pull the first card to set the tone. Once the question is answered, other guests are welcome to ask follow-up questions or add their own thoughts.

I've learned from experience that some people jump right in, while others have to be coaxed. You may even get some pushback from folks who are timid or just private with their thoughts and memories. That's fine—go ahead and let them off the hook.

As the memories, hopes, and dreams begin to spill out in your group, several biblical admonitions will be revealed.

- You may discover ways to "spur one another on toward love and good deeds" (Hebrews 10:24).

- You may uncover new empathy for someone in the room when you "rejoice with those who rejoice, and weep with those who weep" (Romans 12:15 NASB).

- You may find yourself being "harmonious, sympathetic, brotherly, kindhearted, and humble in spirit" (1 Peter 3:8 NASB).

- You may be able to give a friend or family member a new perspective on something that's causing them pain, pointing out that faith makes it possible to "rejoice in our sufferings, knowing that suffering produces endurance, and endurance produces character, and character produces hope" (Romans 5:3-4 ESV).

- You may get proof that there is indeed "a time to weep and a time to laugh, a time to mourn and a time to dance" (Ecclesiastes 3:4).

Do your guests a favor and have a pack of question cards on hand for the next time you experience a lull in your dinner table or party conversation. You may even discover something about yourself.

Checking the List

Jesus used questions to engage the minds of his followers and his detractors, often answering questions with questions. If you want to really show someone you care, ask them thoughtful questions. Then listen!

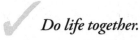 **Do life together.**

WD-40, Duct Tape, Baby Wash, Isopropyl Alcohol, Good Scissors, New Toothbrush, Giant Ziploc Bags, Nail Polish Remover, a Heavy Scotch Tape Dispenser, and Vanilla Ice Cream

As a public service, we're going to take a break from the shopping list that God might have for you and review a few items that very likely belong on your own next shopping list. These frequently overlooked or forgotten items just might make your life a little more pleasant. The hope is that your slightly improved life will spill over into the lives of those around you.

WD-40 and duct tape. There's an old adage among homeowners: "If it moves and it shouldn't, use duct tape. If it doesn't move and it should, use WD-40." Of course, that's not always the case, but it's not far off.

Baby wash. Instead of bars of soap, get an oversized bottle of baby bath soap with a pump top and keep it on the floor of your shower. Great smell. Doesn't dry your skin. No more tears.

Isopropyl alcohol. Moisten a paper towel and clean all kinds of things, including dry-erase boards, venetian blinds, earring backs, and electronics. It can even restore dried-out Sharpies and repel bedbugs.

Nail polish remover. It has even a little more cleaning power than alcohol. Even removes ink stains, permanent marker, and superglue.

Good scissors. Every home needs a pair of good scissors...kept in the same place and returned there after each use.

New toothbrushes. Who doesn't love a new toothbrush?

Ziploc bags. They're not just for sandwiches anymore. They come in a variety of sizes. Packing for a business trip, I fold dress shirts in the two-and-a-half-gallon bag. Track down larger sizes for dust-free, bug-free storage.

Scotch tape dispenser. No reason to mess with flimsy, clear, hand-held tape dispensers. Get a nice heavy one so you can tear off tape with one hand.

Vanilla ice cream. With pie. Sandwiched between chocolate chip cookies. In a fruit smoothie. Swirled with just about anything. Always shopping-list worthy.

Is there an idea here you can use? I hope so. To be clear, this kind of list does not feature any biblical mandates or magic portals to eternity. But there is value here. Think of it this way. By providing you with a few helpful ideas, I've gained just a wee bit of your trust. Later on, when I come alongside you with a spiritual truth that does have eternal consequences, you might think, *This guy hasn't steered me wrong yet.*

Perhaps it's a minor point. In this world, just about everyone has gifts, bits of knowledge, experiences, and commonsense advice worth sharing. But for those who love God and are called according to his purpose, everything we say and do should build bridges and nudge people closer to Jesus. That's why we're here.

So maybe baby wash and ice cream *are* on God's shopping list.

Checking the List

In case you've been feeling small and insignificant, please know that you don't have to spearhead a thirty-city revival campaign to make a difference for Christ. Perhaps the most effective evangelism done today is by those who are simply authentic and sincere with the people they meet every day. Share what works for you. I love Micah 6:8: "What does the LORD require of you? To act justly and to love mercy and to walk humbly with your God."

 Share what you know.

Good Night's Sleep

The little girl next door was my son Alec's best friend in kindergarten. Her family was awesome, and she was a delight. But Mom and Dad were at wits' end because their little angel just wouldn't fall asleep. Come nightfall, this good-natured, smiling girl would become unruly and unreasonable.

As memory serves, these dedicated parents tried all kinds of recommendations and remedies gathered from well-meaning experts, family members, and friends, including lullabies, warm milk, allergy tests, dietary adjustments, stuffed animals, warm blankets, cool breezes, night-lights, and air purifiers.

The only thing that worked was to let her fall asleep in the living room and carefully carry her to bed. Actually, that wasn't a bad solution. When a dad scoops up a sleeping youngster in his strong arms, carries her to her bedroom, lays her gently in bed, and kisses her forehead, all seems right with the world. Still, her parents desperately wanted to solve the mystery.

She wasn't a complainer or even very talkative, so they really couldn't get her to articulate her discomfort or anxiety. That is, until they went to the circus…and she saw the clowns. She was not a happy camper. And she let all three rings know loud and clear.

Coulrophobia is fairly common in young school-age children, but parents often overlook it. Even though they left the big top in a hurry, that young family is grateful the circus came to town, because that night, Mom put two and two together.

It seems one of the first gifts that little girl ever received was a life-like portrait of a clown from her grandparents. The colors were bright. The clown's smile was captivating. It was painted with love. And it was devilishly frightening to a little girl who felt abandoned by her parents in a dark room.

With Mom's discovery, the portrait was removed and the problem was solved. Grandma felt terrible, but it wasn't her fault at all. I'm not sure where the painting ended up.

The entire episode suggests that—if you're a parent—you take a fresh look at the environment in which your children fall asleep. (Or don't fall asleep.)

Paintings of nightmarish, grease-painted figures are not the only possible impediments to sleep. In the dim shadows of the night, even stuffed animals can bring night sweats. At the right angle, cuddly bunnies become attack rabbits. Clothes trees become killer robots. American Girl dolls become armies of zombies. It doesn't take much to imagine where the screenwriters for *Chucky* and *Transformers* found their inspiration. You also have to wonder what was hanging on the walls in young Stephen King's sleep chamber.

Once the young people in your life are safely tucked in, I encourage you to consider your own sleep patterns. Like most adults, you're probably not getting that eight hours of recuperating slumber, are you?

What's keeping you awake at night? What's on your walls, in your dreams, or on your mind as you attempt to drift off to sleep?

For kids, it's the stuff that makes them feel unsafe over which they have no control. For adults, it's also the stuff that makes us feel unsafe, but the insomnia comes because we feel like we should be able to have some kind of control. After all, we're adults. We are no longer afraid of clowns, snakes under the bed, or monsters in the closet. Right?

Unfortunately, the stuff keeping so many adults awake is not imaginary. We've got bills to pay, bosses to placate, children to worry about, careers to reassess, apologies to make, addictions to fend off, and hot water heaters to replace. Our migraines, deadlines, cravings, leaking roofs, and nasty neighbors are very real.

What's keeping you awake won't disappear simply by taking down a piece of bad art. The worrisome thoughts and night terrors don't go away that easily. And it's every night.

What could possibly be on God's shopping list that helps you find sweet release and sweet dreams? Well, there's the physical side. A new pillow or mattress might be in order. You may need to do something about the temperature of the room, the flickering streetlight, the creaks of a settling house, or the sirens in the distance. A ceiling fan, space heater, sleep mask, earplugs, or sound machine, perhaps?

Nicotine, caffeine, heavy meals, chronic pain, and allergies can cause irregular sleep patterns. Sleep experts suggest you put your smartphone in another room.

God cares that you get a good night's sleep.

The entirety of Proverbs 3 is a wonderful passage extolling the virtue of seeking wisdom, trusting God, and giving generously. Verses 21-26 speak to how God's presence and wisdom remove fear of sudden disaster or ruin and ultimately provide for sleep that's sweet.

> My son, do not let wisdom and understanding out of
> your sight,
> preserve sound judgment and discretion;
> they will be life for you,
> an ornament to grace your neck.
> Then you will go on your way in safety,
> and your foot will not stumble.
> When you lie down, you will not be afraid;
> when you lie down, your sleep will be sweet.
> Have no fear of sudden disaster
> or of the ruin that overtakes the wicked,

for the LORD will be at your side
and will keep your foot from being snared.

Maybe you're in the middle of a spiritual battle but can't admit
it. With all the challenges on your heart and mind—from broken
finances to broken friendships—are you trying to handle them all by
yourself? Proverbs 3 might hold the answer to your worst nightmare.
The Lord is already at your side. All you have to do is turn to him and
take full advantage of the sound judgment, discretion, wisdom, and
understanding he's offering you.

Checking the List

What do you fear? Turn those fears over to the one who loves you
most.

Wishing you sweet dreams.

~~Sex~~

Sex should not be on any shopping list. Because sex should never be for sale. I hope you agree.

That definitive statement includes prostitution, sex trafficking, pornography, strip clubs, and any transaction in which sex or the idea of sex is bought and sold.

But let's not stop there. Let's all agree that our culture has made sex a commodity, and it's used to sell everything from perfume to chainsaws. In many ways, you can't fault marketers. Sex is a powerful force, and it's easy to attract attention to a product or service by triggering carnal emotions through any of the five senses.

Advertisers know sex sells. But that does not give us permission to sell sex.

Why? Because sex is more than a biological function. Sex is a gift. A gift from the Creator and a gift that husbands and wives can give each other in the context of a committed marriage relationship. It's countercultural to say this, but opening that gift at the right time with the right person provides an umbrella of protection and provision that is impossible to replicate through any other human endeavor.

Sex is that powerful. That valuable. And there's no price tag you can put on it.

Saving sex until after the wedding protects men and women from guilt, disease, unwanted pregnancy, comparisons with other partners, and heartbreak. More than that, giving that gift one time to one person provides a unique, intimate awareness of how to meet each other's needs outside the bedroom. It's like a secret shared by just the two of you.

The idea of giving yourself only to each other—forsaking all others—discovering together what love really means as husband and wife is why the Bible teaches, "Marriage should be honored by all, and the marriage bed kept pure" (Hebrews 13:4). It's not just to protect us; it's to provide the kind of love that far too many couples never experience.

All that being said, because of the nature of our culture, you may have had sexual experiences outside of marriage. The reasons are many. The lust of youth. Peer pressure. Bad decisions fueled by alcohol, anger, jealousy, and curiosity. Often unmarried couples keep pushing the boundaries because they were never taught otherwise. And the cultural climate provides no reason to slow down. Of course, anyone forced, coerced, or manipulated into a sexual encounter will have to recover from that emotional wound to once again see sex as a gift to share with a beloved partner. Even within marriages, sex can deteriorate from a gift to a bargaining tool or dreaded responsibility.

The result for too many people is that sex is no longer treasured or cherished. That's what happens when something of value is forfeited carelessly, casually, criminally, or thoughtlessly.

Restating the obvious, I believe God would never suggest anyone should ever *shop* for sex. In a dating, courting, or marriage relationship, you may experience and pursue friendship, devotion, affection, and romance. But God's design for sex is a separate category. Beyond reproduction, it's a physical act created to connect couples emotionally, spiritually, and permanently.

Maybe think of it this way. Respect, love, shared joy, and steadfast commitment lead to sex. Which leads to even more respect, love, shared joy, and steadfast commitment.

Checking the List

An unforgettable verse appears in the Bible three times—in Genesis 2, Matthew 19, and Ephesians 5—reminding us that "a man leaves his father and mother and is united to his wife, and they become one flesh." Becoming one flesh means your hearts, needs, desires, and entire lives become inseparable. That's why sex just isn't for sale.

 *The two shall become one.*

Apple Butter, Nesquik, and Hostess Cherry Pies

These three items are probably *not* on your shopping list, but they will always be on mine. Each one comes with an amusing memory. As humans relate with each other, we share memories to connect, make friends, find soulmates, and eventually look to the future.

So. Three quick stories about three items found on the shelves of most grocery stores and, quite often, in my shopping cart.

Apple butter. When I was eleven, my brother and I went to Chin-Be-Gota Boy Scout camp in north central Wisconsin for a week. It rained every day, all day. At a camp focusing on outdoor activities, that meant there wasn't much to do. But at least we had apple butter.

Somehow, our family had never discovered apple butter, and therein lies the punchline of this tale. At Chin-Be-Gota, breakfast, lunch, and dinner were served at very specific times. Otherwise, the mess hall was closed. Except for—you guessed it—an endless supply of white bread and apple butter. Apple butter saved our week. For that reason, Mark and I thought it was the most delicious food product ever created. We couldn't wait to get home to our warm, dry beds and to introduce our uneducated and deprived family to the wondrousness of apple butter.

Our first day home from Boy Scout camp, we insisted Mom take us to the supermarket. Mark and I ran to the jelly and jam aisle. And there it was! We had walked right past this amazing product hundreds of times. At home, we eagerly spread the sweet brown nectar on slices of Wonder Bread, chomped on it with great anticipation…and were violently disappointed. It wasn't good. It tasted a little like the delicacy we had discovered just a week earlier, but without rain dripping off pine trees, pitiful bouts of homesickness, and damp socks, apple butter had lost its appeal.

Decades later, I have a new appreciation for apple butter. It is what it is. Nothing special, really. Except for me, it's a memory jogger that takes me back to those days of youth when everything was much simpler. And I learned an important lesson about expectations, appreciation, and the comforts of home.

Hostess Cherry Pies. Growing up, after church service it was customary for my family to stop by the local Open Pantry mini-mart. (This was back when the big supermarkets were closed on Sundays.) We'd pick up a few necessities to get us through the afternoon, knowing we'd sit down later that evening to our other Sunday family ritual of roast beef, mashed potatoes, and carrots.

At the mini-mart, each of us kids got to pick a packaged dessert that would go into our brown bag lunch for school the next day. My siblings' choices would vary from week to week: Twinkies, Sno Balls, Dolly Madison cakes, and so on. But I stuck with the tried and true Hostess Cherry Pie in the sealed red wax rectangular package.

Sitting at my desk Monday morning, I couldn't wait for lunch. Roast beef sandwich and cherry pie. I never did tell my mom that I always peeled off the soggy piece of lettuce she had carefully placed on the sandwich the night before. Still, Monday lunches are a fond memory worth sharing.

Unlike apple butter, roast beef sandwiches and Hostess Cherry Pies are as delicious as ever. Maybe more so. I wonder why that is?

Nesquik. Pushing the cart one afternoon during a family grocery shopping expedition, I deliberately pulled a container of Nestle's Quik (the name changed to Nesquik in 1999) off the shelf and placed it in the basket. We were out of Quik, and it seemed like a reasonable purchase. Unfortunately, that's not the way shopping worked in our family. Unless we were told to track something down, only Mom or Dad placed items in the basket. My dad noticed. He said quite sternly, "We don't need that." I clearly remember the store, the aisle, my father's expression, and my sincere reply: "I don't ask for much."

He was just a bit stunned. He paused, knowing I was right. And he said the only thing he could say: "All right then." We bought the Quik. Well, the story has become legend in our family. My dad thoroughly enjoyed recalling the day Jay stood up to him at the Kroger. In addition, even decades later, he would bring gifts of Nestle's Quik to my house just to make sure my supply didn't run low.

Looking back, he must have truly appreciated the moment, seeing his son be respectfully assertive and speak his mind. That's a trait any father would want to see in his kids.

I believe God's shopping list for us would include items that evoke memories and connect generations. Especially if those purchases lead to shared stories. Maybe yours go something like this…

"Even though she knew I liked plain M&M's, my grandmother always bought peanut. It was a running joke we had."

"I survived on ramen noodles through college, and just to remain humble, I make sure to keep a few packages in my cupboard."

"On the drive up to the lake, I still stop in the same town at the same store to buy a couple comic books. It's a tradition that goes back to when I was seven or eight."

According to Proverbs 10:7 (esv), "The memory of the righteous is a blessing." Now that verse doesn't claim all memories are pleasant and joy filled. But it does suggest that God has brought you to this place with those experiences for a reason and that he wants to bless our lives. There's great security in that understanding. We should be cognizant of our past so that we can look to the future and ask, "God, I trust you. What do you have next for me?" That answer may come more quickly if you're dining on ramen noodles or spreading apple butter on a slice of bread.

Checking the List

If you can't think of any product-related memories, go open your fridge or pantry. You bought that brand of mustard, toothpaste, dish soap, or cereal for a reason. Share that story with a friend or family member today.

 Reflect on your past to better discern your future.

Books to Give Away

I've written several books on fathering. One of my biggest thrills is when a grandfather buys one of my books to give to his son or son-in-law. That older gentleman is not just giving an encouraging gift. He's resourcing that younger dad, confirming the importance of intentional fathering, and impacting his grandkids and generations to come.

My wife likes to hold babies, which is convenient because babies like to be held. Rita rocked and cuddled our five kids and is an outspoken advocate regarding the importance of nurturing newborns. That's one of the reasons we've also welcomed ten foster babies into our home. Several of those newborns came from moms who were addicts, and our entire family learned how to swaddle those little ones as they trembled through cocaine withdrawal.

Several years ago, Rita happened across a book titled *You Are My World: How a Parent's Love Shapes a Baby's Mind* by Amy Hatkoff. That book exactly reflected Rita's heart and experience. It's a quick read with many engaging photos. Using love, logic, and science, the author confirms the importance of early attachment, reading your baby's cues, and entering their world. We ordered a case of that book (the publisher gave us a nice discount), and Rita makes sure every new mom she hears about receives a copy. Including our own daughters-in-law.

Another book I have given away at least a dozen times to boys who seem to need a bit of encouragement is *The Phantom Tollbooth* written by Norton Juster and illustrated by Jules Feiffer. It was the first chapter book I read back in grade school and has become a substantial part of our family lore. The 1966 book opens with a bored young man named Milo and soon whisks him into the Lands Beyond. He joins forces with a watchdog named Tock and meets unforgettable characters like the Whether Man, King Azaz, and the Spelling Bee. His mission is to climb the Mountains of Ignorance, conquer a slew of unconventional demons, and rescue the Princesses Rhyme and Reason.

One Christmas, my daughter bought me a collector's edition of *The Phantom Tollbooth* signed by the author and illustrator. An illustration in my very first book, *Once Upon a Tandem*, was inspired by one of Feiffer's illustrations. My eldest, Alec, was named after one of the characters in the book. I especially love giving away copies to boys also named Alec.

The best books to give away are ones you've read and loved. For sure, some books you'll want to keep on your own shelf for future reference or to reread. But most of the time, when you finish a book, the best course of action is to give it to someone who came to mind while you were reading it. No strings attached.

Finally, the Payleitner family has also given away Bibles. It's encouraging to think that a Bible we've pulled off our shelves or purchased specifically for a friend or acquaintance might be impacting and guiding that person's life this very moment. Psalm 119:105 promises, "Your word is a lamp for my feet, a light on my path."

You can't go wrong giving away a copy of God's Word. One at a time to people with whom you cross paths or by making a financial gift to a ministry like Bible League International or Oasis International Limited. As the prophet said, "it always produces fruit" (Isaiah 55:11 NLT).

Checking the List

As an author, I've given away hundreds of books. Sometimes to strangers in restaurants and parking lots. But I confess, most of the times when I give away a book, it's a promotional copy or a gift to a pastor or event planner hoping they might invite me to speak at a retreat, breakfast, or Sunday service. So that kind of book distribution probably shouldn't even be mentioned. Especially in a chapter encouraging you to buy books and give them away out of the goodness of your heart.

 Read. Share. Grow.

Rodent Hairs, Fly Eggs, Mold, and Insect Fragments

You don't have to add these food items to your shopping list. You probably already have them if you have any peanut butter, ground cinnamon, macaroni, canned tomatoes, or wheat flour in your refrigerator or cabinets.

But don't worry about this. The *Defect Level Handbook* published by the US Food and Drug Administration only allows certain "levels of natural or unavoidable defects in foods for human use that present no health hazard." If you trust the government, you can be confident these minimal amounts can be ingested with complete safety because the FDA employees who monitor these acceptable food defects are described as "technical and regulatory experts in filth and extraneous materials."[4]

Without getting too grossed out, allow me to list of a few of the foreign substances that are permitted in your favorite grocery items.

Apple butter: up to five or more whole or equivalent insects per 100 grams.

Frozen broccoli: up to sixty or more aphids or mites per 100 grams.

Ground paprika: average mold count of up to 20 percent.

Ground oregano: up to five rodent hairs per 10 grams.

Peanut butter: up to thirty or more insect fragments per 100 grams.

Canned citrus fruit juices: five or more fly eggs per 250 milliliters.

The handbook includes dozens of other standards, but you get the idea.

Now here's the challenge with this chapter. Don't let this information keep you from buying peanut butter and orange juice. Because really, it's not a big deal. As a matter of fact, there's a sense that eating slightly defective food is good for you. Not munching on dirt. Not drinking milk that's gone bad. But ingesting a few microbes, bacteria, fungi, or dust bunnies could very well be a good thing.

In their book *Dirt Is Good*, Dr. Jack Gilbert and Dr. Rob Knight describe the 40 trillion bacterial cells and genes in the human body acting in concert to form a microbiome that promotes healthy digestion and a stronger immune system. Recent studies suggest you should throw away your antimicrobial soap, new parents don't have to sterilize baby bottles, and kisses from the neighbor's dog are perfectly acceptable.

Because I'm not a doctor, I need to stop here and maybe even backtrack on my medical advice. My lawyers also want me to tell you to consult your own doctor before eating dirt or tossing out everything in your pantry.

Here's the not-so-surprising point. Let's all pledge to eat healthy and get some exercise. We know what that means. Less sugar, fat, and carbs. More fresh vegetables, lean meats, and whole grains. Less sitting around and sleeping in. More walking, biking, stretching, and swimming.

That would be a lifestyle choice, not an obsession. Worrying about less-than-perfect peanut butter, sterilizing every dropped pacifier, or never again eating frozen broccoli are mistakes in more ways than one. Such worry distracts us from good stuff, stirs up fear about inconsequential stuff, and takes our eyes off the prize that is eternity with the Savior.

Besides, worrying is pointless. In Matthew 6:27, Jesus states the obvious: "Can any one of you by worrying add a single hour to your life?"

Considering all the government statistics and medical advice, it occurs to me that this chapter may be inadvertently *adding* to your list of things to worry about. Allow me to double down on my assertion: Small amounts of stuff that your mother said was bad for you is probably not. And may even be good for you. Okay?

Checking the List

Worry only about stuff that really matters. If it does matter, and if you can do something about it, then do. But for the most part, you'll want to "cast all your anxiety on him because he cares for you" (1 Peter 5:7).

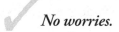 *No worries.*

A Coke to Share at McDonald's

In the late 1980s, McDonald's and most other fast-food chains began offering free refills for dine-in customers. Two unfortunate things resulted.

The first is that just about everyone who ordered a soft drink got a refill. Why wouldn't you? The fountain Cokes at McDonald's are just about the best drink in the world. Especially on a hot day. Plus, that refill is free! Suddenly, millions of Americans were consuming twice as much Coca-Cola as they were before the new policy. (FYI, there are 220 calories in a medium Coke at McDonalds. And those are empty, bloat-inducing calories. Doing the math, that's 440 calories if you include that refill. And 660 if you refill twice. Burp.)

Enough about that. I love McDonald's. I recommend McDonald's. If you can navigate their touch-screen ordering, I know you'll enjoy the McDonald's experience. Even more so if you go easy on the soft drinks.

The second and most significant unfortunate thing about free refills for dine-in customers is that you can no longer go to your favorite fast-food joint with your significant other and share a Coke.

Why? Because it's stealing.

Stay with me here. Back in the day, you and your best guy or gal could go into a Mickey D's, order a large fries and large Coke—with two straws—and sit in a booth making small talk for a good half hour. When the fries and Coke were gone, that was that. You might hang out for a while longer. But the transaction was clean and innocent. You bought X amount of food and drink for X amount of dollars and consumed it honorably.

Today, one of you would jump up and cross to the fountain drink dispenser to get a refill. And suddenly the drink you bought for one is being consumed by two. Ergo, stealing.

You may disagree. But really, there's no ambiguity here. You paid for a soft drink for one person. And two people are drinking.

I can hear your arguments.

"It's not like I'm stealing a car or even a cheeseburger." Sorry. Stealing is stealing.

"They make so much money on pop. It's like two cents for the syrup, and the rest is just carbonated water." Quantity is irrelevant when it comes to the definition of stealing.

"The girl at the counter making minimum wage doesn't care." Still stealing.

"We're only getting one refill, and one refill is reflected in the price." An interesting argument, but you purchased a drink for one, not a drink for two.

"I drank most of it. My girlfriend only had a sip." One little sip? Really? Okay, that's probably not stealing.

Does this sound all too legalistic? Yeah, it does. But we cannot deny that there is a right and wrong. Denial or ignorance doesn't change facts.

Just to be clear, this chapter is not about our country's legal system. Very few people have gone to jail for stealing a Coke at McDonald's. Probably no one has gone to jail for *sharing* a Coke at McDonald's. We're not talking about felonies and misdemeanors here. Again, we're talking about right and wrong.

Here are other examples that may seem like gray areas but really aren't.

- Taking packets of sugar, Sweet'n Low, or Equal from restaurant table caddies to use at home.
- Taking hotel towels, pillows, coffee mugs, lightbulbs, or hangers. (Shampoo is fair game.)
- Tipping less than 15 percent at a sit-down restaurant unless the service was absolutely horrible.
- Taking office supplies from work.
- Punching out for a workmate who left before the end of the day.
- Padding an expense account.

Yikes. This list could go on for a while. But here again is the point. There is a right and a wrong. And the decision about what is right and wrong cannot be left to us. There are several schools of thought on how to determine if something is good or bad. Sinful or not.

Based on consequences. If there's no penalty or no victim, then it's okay. Really? Let's all agree that something is not okay just because you didn't get caught. If the hotel or your boss looks the other way or doesn't press charges, that doesn't mean that stealing from the hotel or your company is not stealing.

Based on personal virtue. If it doesn't bother my conscience, then it's okay. So you can do something terrible—really terrible—and if you don't feel bad, it can't possibly be a sin. Please, let's agree that the definition of sin cannot be left up to individual standards.

Based on group standards. If the culture accepts it, then it's okay. That's just as bad as using personal standards—maybe worse. Entire cultures and governments have been perfectly fine with the idea of exterminating entire races, killing unborn children, sacrificing virgins in volcanoes, or chopping off the hands of convicted thieves.

Based on God's character. Now we're on to something. God is truth, so lying is wrong. God is life, so killing is wrong. God is just, so stealing is wrong. God is merciful, so holding on to anger is wrong. God is loving, so hate is wrong.

Based on God's laws. A great starting place is the Ten Commandments, but Jesus may have had the final word in this famous and relevant passage.

> "Teacher, which is the greatest commandment in the Law?"
> Jesus replied: "'Love the Lord your God with all your heart and with all your soul and with all your mind.' This is the first and greatest commandment. And the second is like it: 'Love your neighbor as yourself.' All the Law and the Prophets hang on these two commandments" (Matthew 22:36-40).

God's shopping list may include things that are morally neutral. Like an alarm clock, dining room table, or telescope. But he's not going to have us pursuing goals, exhibiting morals, or making purchases that dishonor his name.

Considering the state of today's moral culture, what the world says matters very little. Sometimes that means we stand against the culture or rethink some long-held personal convictions. We also need to take the time to know his express written laws and get to know him in a personal way so we can reflect his character and hear his voice.

Checking the List

We all stumble. Our immediate response is often to make excuses or justify our actions. It's a human response. But those who call themselves Christians need to hold ourselves to a standard the world may not understand. The smallest of sins doesn't lead to God loving you less. But it does break his heart.

 Reflect the character of God in all you do.

Space Heater or Box Fan

Let's talk a bit about compromise. Now, you might think that for people doing life together—married couples, roommates, employees sharing office space—compromise would be a good thing. Sorry, but quite often compromise either isn't possible or simply means that no one gets their way. You're shooting for a win-win outcome, but compromise often turns out to be a lose-lose.

If one wants to set the thermostat at sixty-six degrees and the other wants seventy-four degrees, the compromise would be to set it at seventy degrees. And then neither is comfy.

If both employees want to sit facing the window, it might be possible to arrange the desks so that they each have sideways views of the outside world. But maybe not.

If eight office workers request a vacation day on the Friday after Thanksgiving, the boss could have everyone come in for one hour. But does that compromise make sense?

If he likes Mexican food and she likes Italian, the compromise position would be to go to Denny's or Applebee's, where he can order nachos and she can order spaghetti and meatballs. But really, wouldn't you rather hit up that awesome local restaurant with the authentic Mexican or Italian cuisine?

If he wants to live in Seattle and she wants to live in Miami, the compromise would be Wichita. But would either person be happy there? Well, maybe. But that's not the point.

If a married couple gets a $4,000 windfall, a decision needs to be made whether to do a household project, pay off a debt, or take a dream vacation. There may be some disagreement.

So what's a better solution than compromise?

Sometimes, you can look for and find an easy answer. If he likes crunchy and she likes creamy, don't take turns and wait until one peanut butter jar is empty. Buy two jars!

Instead of declaring thermostat wars, set the temperature for one of you and invest in a space heater or box fan for the office worker or spouse who's too cold or too hot. A cuddly comforter might help as well.

What to do with an unexpected four grand is not something to decide on a whim. Talk it over until you're on the same page. After talking respectfully, you'll realize that replacing the broken water heater is probably more urgent than installing the crown molding. Paying off a high-interest loan would likely take precedent over a vacation. Unless you really, really need a vacation.

The same approach must be taken with where to live. There are a thousand deciding considerations, so take the time to get them all out on the table. Some factors will be practical. Some emotional. Some nonnegotiable. You're not bargaining; you're making a wise decision. Pray together. For this next season of life, the place to call home will become clear.

Often the best solution is for you—yes you, dear reader—to make a sacrificial gift of the decision. Give Sally the desk facing the window. If it can fit in your schedule, volunteer to work so others can enjoy the day off. Without delivering a shred of guilt, make reservations at your spouse's favorite restaurant.

Seeking God's will—in private or with the other party—may be the best approach to any potential conflict or difference of opinion. After all, you're looking for wisdom, and James 1:5 promises, "If any of you lacks wisdom, you should ask God, who gives generously to all without finding fault, and it will be given to you."

In the end, make it a gift. Perhaps done in secret. You also might want to consider these three cautions: Don't allow yourself to become a doormat. Don't grumble as you give your gift. And don't set yourself to be a grand martyr.

Instead, see if you can be a blessing to others and get joy out of the experience. Putting others first honors God. "Submit to one another out of reverence for Christ" (Ephesians 5:21).

Especially at work, you may be able to use the entire experience as a gentle witnessing tool:

"Well, that was awful nice of you."

"To tell you the truth, I prayed about it. And God nudged me this way. And I'm glad to do it."

Checking the List

Of course, compromise is complicated. In some situations, it may result in a perfect arrangement in which everyone feels good about the final decision. But sometimes there are sacrifices to be made. Let's honor that. In the end, let's also be aware that we have a personal responsibility to try to calm any storm of divisiveness or controversy. "If it is possible, as far as it depends on you, live at peace with everyone" (Romans 12:18).

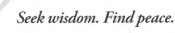 *Seek wisdom. Find peace.*

Christian Bumper Stickers

Are you a fan of evangelism by pithy statement? I don't think I am. Here is a batch of clever bumper-sticker-length declarations that I really cannot recommend for your Mercedes, Maserati, or mini-van. Some are clever or amusing. Some may even be true. But I'm pretty sure they are not on God's shopping list for most people.

God's not dead. I spoke with him this morning.

No God, no peace. Know God, know peace.

Jesus loves you, but I'm his favorite.

If God is your copilot, switch seats.

Honk if you love Jesus. Text if you want to see him.

My boss is a Jewish carpenter.

God answers knee-mail.

Got Jesus?

Life is fragile. Handle with prayer.

Today's weather forecast: Jesus reigns.

This car is prayer-conditioned.

Jesus built us a bridge with two boards and three nails.

Warning: In case of rapture, this car will be unmanned.

God allows U-turns.

#Believe

Don't follow me, follow Jesus.

Christians aren't perfect, just forgiven.

If you have one of these clever phrases stuck to your rear bumper, please don't feel like you should scrape it off based on this chapter. Same goes for your imitation metallic Jesus fish or window decal with a crown of thorns or praying silhouette.

I could be dead wrong. There's a chance your car decoration might occasionally lead another driver to think new thoughts on who Jesus is and how God might really have a plan for each of us. But there's also a chance bumper stickers with witty slogans and easy-sounding answers will have a negative impact. Especially if you're breaking speed limits and cutting people off in traffic.

I'm also afraid some bumper-sticker readers might be a bit insulted by the idea that a decision so big—someone's spiritual beliefs—can be reduced to a few witty or rhyming words. Provoking someone to groan, roll their eyes, or shake their head is not going to open the door to many meaningful conversations about God's love, Jesus's sacrifice, or the power of the Holy Spirit.

The one possible category of bumper stickers or window decals that might provoke some reasonable curiosity could be simple Scripture references. For instance, "John 3:16," "Romans 5:8," "Joshua 24:15," "Acts 16:31," or "Psalm 23." To me, those cryptic words and numbers might create questions in the mind of the reader. *What does that mean? And what do Bible readers know that I don't?*

I recall watching a football game at a family restaurant when a group of fans behind the goalposts held up a large banner that simply read "John 3:16." A casual friend who knew I was a church attender asked what it meant. We had a worthwhile discussion that went on past the end of the commercial break.

I'm a former ad man. I wrote headlines and commercials for airlines, supermarket chains, canned vegetables, adult beverages, books, and Bibles. I appreciate the good turn of a phrase. But being clever doesn't draw people to the gospel or new life in Christ. Only God does that. And he uses his Word.

Isaiah 55:11 (NLT) promises that when God sends out his word, it always has an impact: "It is the same with my word. I send it out, and it always produces fruit. It will accomplish all I want it to, and it will prosper everywhere I send it."

With that in mind, let's leave this item as optional on the shopping list God has for you. With these three conditions: You commit to driving mostly within the traffic laws, you choose a bumper sticker that really reflects your heart, and you develop a nice little speech you can share with anyone who asks you about what it means.

Checking the List

We all need to develop a few triggers that lead to polite and sincere spiritual conversations. "How was your weekend?" can lead to talking about the sermon you heard last Sunday. "Read any good books lately?" can lead to a nice conversation about this book or, even better, the Bible. "What's with that bumper sticker?" could open the door to a fun exchange about a simple biblical truth.

Words matter. Context also matters.

The Entire Wendy's Dollar Menu—Twice

This purchase is probably not specifically on God's shopping list for you. It is merely an excuse to tell one of my favorite stories. If it inspires you to be a little sillier or make outrageous memories with your family or friends, that's a bonus.

My sons Randall and Max are three and a half years apart. Of my five kids, they were the most antagonistic toward each other from toddler age through middle school. When Randall headed off to college, suddenly Max missed his sparring partner. As their time together became more precious, their sibling rivalry somehow morphed into a deep and abiding friendship. As a dad, I felt blessed to see it.

Still, the competitiveness remained.

One perfect summer evening, the boys were extolling the virtue, value, and tastiness of items on the Wendy's dollar menu. Somehow speculation began regarding whether it was possible for a single individual to consume one of everything on that menu, including three different burgers, one chicken sandwich, a five-piece order of chicken nuggets, a cup of chili, a small order of fries, a baked potato, a salad, a Frosty, and a beverage of choice—all in one sitting.

Somehow that idea morphed into pitting the seventeen-year-old against the twenty-year-old in a contest of wills and stomach stretching. Somehow Dad paid for the entire event.

The folks at Wendy's should be glad we didn't use their dining room. Instead, the sacks of fast food were spread out on our picnic table while friends and family gathered for the unlikely competitive feast. Details are sketchy. I do remember it wasn't pretty. Years later, both boys claim some kind of victory. But the truth is Randall and Max both wisely gave up with a few burgers still left in their wrappings.

It was probably the best $22 plus tax I spent that summer. The howls of laughter still echo through our backyard and family room.

Bragging rights remain unclaimed. But I'll claim victory for all parents, ringmasters, and visionaries who encourage occasional reckless behavior. The sheer joy of allowing such a foolhardy event to take place is a reward too often missed by the uptight and priggish.

Thinking back, there may be a biblical principle to be gained by all of this. The overarching theme of the book of Ecclesiastes seems to be that the meaning of life cannot be found in many of the typical pursuits of humankind. That includes knowledge, money, pleasure, work, prestige, and power. Those outcomes may not be evil, but if they are the goal, the result will inevitably be disappointment and disillusionment. Our purpose is to fix our eyes on eternity with Christ, which is the path to an abundant life.

You may be surprised to hear that enjoying life is on God's shopping list for us. In Ecclesiastes 8:15, he grants us permission to experience merriment—eating, drinking, and mirth—under certain conditions.

> So I commend the enjoyment of life, because there is nothing better for a person under the sun than to eat and drink and be glad. Then joy will accompany them in their toil all the days of the life God has given them under the sun.

Notice that joy is a gift from God as well as the result of hard work. Thinking back, the summertime Wendy's feast was frivolous. But what made it possible—and fun—was that Max, Randall, and the entire crew assembled that evening were not freeloading vagabonds piling on one reckless activity after another. It was a well-earned yet spontaneous moment of silliness.

I hope you get a chance to enjoy a similar experience in the very near future.

Checking the List

Joy, laughter, and delight are results, not primary causes. Such benefits are the rewards of living a life pleasing to the Creator of the universe.

 Earn a joy-filled life.

Empty Notebook

C all it a diary. Or spiritual log. Or prayer journal.

You can write in sharpened pencil or retractable gel pen. Or tap your phone. Or set up a file folder on your laptop.

Feel free to record page after page of thoughtful prose with perfect grammar, capturing your deepest thoughts and emotions to be referenced often and saved to inspire future generations. Or scribble blurbs and one-word notes that only you can decipher when you turn back to that date.

Crack open that notebook at scheduled times every morning, every night, once a week, or spontaneously ten times a day as you wait for deliveries, customer service, transportation, or the after-school pickup. Keep that spiral notebook next to your Bible or maintain that digital document on your favorite screen-bearing device.

You get the idea. However you set up and use your notebook / prayer journal, you will want to make sure it meshes with your lifestyle. Make it easy to access and reference.

What are you making notes about? Anything you want, really. If you've ever kept any kind of diary, you know how fun it is to go back and reflect on those fleeting moments of life that otherwise would be mostly a blur of memories. A walk with a friend when secrets were revealed. A word of hope meant just for you from a radio preacher. A discovery that still affects your life today: finding that quiet bench in the park, reading a new author with a fresh voice, or trying a flavor of hot beverage for the first time. You'll definitely want to log your memories of that life-changing day that included a huge disappointment counterbalanced by a tremendous life victory.

When you put dates beside journal entries, it's amazing how often extraordinary life events are clustered together. Without the journal, you would have forgotten how the new puppy, your first iPhone, and your best friend's medical diagnosis all came the same week that Nana passed away. Remember that avalanche of emotions?

But the real reason to keep a notebook is to record your prayers. Small ones and large ones. Prayers that come to you once in an instant or prayers that come back to your mind and heart over and over for an extended period. Prayers that seem selfish. Prayers that are gracious, generous, and altruistic.

The reason to record your prayers is so you can track how they are answered. And get ready to be surprised. Because God always answers sincere, selfless prayers of faithful believers.

"If you believe, you will receive whatever you ask for in prayer" (Matthew 21:22).

"The prayer of a righteous person is powerful and effective" (James 5:16).

"If you remain in me and my words remain in you, ask whatever you wish, and it will be done for you" (John 15:7).

"When you ask, you do not receive, because you ask with wrong motives, that you may spend what you get on your pleasures" (James 4:3).

Reviewing these passages, you'll see that when you bring your requests to the throne of God, there's a bit of a proviso or stipulation attached. Want your prayers answered? Then believe in God and his plan, be righteous (even in your sinful condition), remain in God's Word (the Bible), and make sure your motives are less about you and more about others.

Searching Scriptures for more hints on effective prayer, you'll find there's an advantage to being persistent, humble, unpretentious, and even confident. There's even biblical evidence that we should sometimes pray in specifics. That goes against our human instincts sometimes. But Jesus wants you to articulate the specific desires of our heart. As recorded in Mark 10:46-52, Jesus responds to a nonspecific plea for mercy from Bartimaeus by asking, "What do you want me to do for you?"

So go ahead and attach a deadline to that prayer for a job at a certain company. Ask for healing for a specific malady so you can partake in a future event. Pray for that friend to face that clear-cut challenge with grace and courage. When we define and focus our prayers, that means we have thought about who we are and what's important. We're relating to God not as a giant vending machine in the sky but as a loving Father who cares about our welfare and influence.

As you may have heard before, God will answer your prayers with a yes, no, or wait. A fourth response might be, "My child, please reconsider your prayer because your request is outside my will for your life."

Perhaps one of the best reasons to explicitly record your prayers is so you can check them off as they are answered. After you've been journaling your prayers, you will be astounded at God's loving responses. Pray according to God's will, and you will find yourself gleefully realizing he is listening, he does care, and prayer does make a difference.

Checking the List

The act of writing your hopes, dreams, desires, and prayers creates a powerful awareness of how God has gifted you and set before you a life of impact and reward. Often it requires actual written words to convert thoughts into actions.

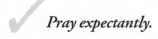 ***Pray expectantly.***

Things Used Once

Have you noticed that on eBay and other for-sale-by-owner sites, quite a few items are described as "like new"? That's because people buy stuff they think they need but only use once. Then that overpriced item sits in their garage, basement, workshop, attic, or spare bedroom for a year or two before they finally realize they will never use it again.

Examples? A handy homeowner decides he needs to take down one mostly dead tree, so he buys a $200 chainsaw and $350 log splitter. Two weeks later the project is finished, and there are no other trees on his property to fell or logs to split.

Throwing a bridal shower, you spend $140 on a top-notch chocolate fountain. It's funny because a running joke between you and your best friend has always been her obsession with chocolate. The fountain is a smash hit, but now what?

For your church children's ministry, you volunteer to host a backyard movie night and invest $300 in a sixteen-foot inflatable movie screen and $200 on a popcorn cart. Despite the rain, the event is a highlight of the summer. But now you don't know what to do with your bulky purchases.

For more examples, just page through the *Sharper Image* catalog.

Actually, don't do that. Because you'll start finding things that are expensive, not necessities, and very likely to be used only a handful of times. Or they're not nearly as gratifying as you had hoped. Skimming through a recent issue, you can't miss the massage chairs, hover boards, air purifiers, golf simulators, fat-reduction systems, and quite a few high-tech gadgets that clearly have more appeal on the printed page (and in our imagination) than in real life.

So what's a better option than purchasing costly and bulky items you'll use once and store forever? A little creativity and common sense will go a long way here.

Borrow. Before buying a toboggan or popcorn maker, see if you can borrow one from your friend or neighbor. Same with expensive specialty tools. There's a good chance someone in your neighborhood owns a chainsaw, wheelbarrow, rototiller, pole saw, and so on. Just make sure to return it promptly and in good condition.

Rent. Party stores have sturdy and user-friendly chocolate fountains, tents, cabanas, bounce houses, frozen-drink machines, cotton candy machines, and more. General merchandise rental outlets have just about anything you can imagine for once-in-a-lifetime parties, seasonal yard work, and home-repair projects. After all, do you really want to own a professional-grade wallpaper steamer or floor sander?

Group purchase. If you're in a group of friends that entertain occasionally, there's no reason all of you need a crystal punch bowl with six dozen glasses or any of the other party gear mentioned earlier. Same with power tools used once a year. Especially in tight-knit neighborhoods, tools for major outdoor projects should be shared. If you get really organized, you may figure out a way to split the cost on the original purchase, upkeep, and replacement. That's the kind of cooperation that helps neighbors know and appreciate each other.

Buy and donate. There may be some tools or event purchases that could be used repeatedly by a church, school, youth center, or other nonprofit. If you've gotten your money's worth, give it away.

Like much of the financial implications of this book, the point is to be a good steward of your resources and possessions. Maybe you *should* own a couple of these big-ticket, rarely used items. Spending several hundred dollars on a youth event in your backyard might be the best investment you ever make. Especially if a bevy of new kids get plugged into a thriving youth program at your church. That rototiller may get pulled out of your backyard shed just once a year, but spending a weekend every spring helping your entire neighborhood loosen the soil in their vegetable gardens can be an outreach that reaps a fall harvest. And a spiritual harvest.

These kinds of purchases cross your mind more often than we imagine. *Wouldn't it be nice if we had a...?* I think God would want you to be mindful and prayerful. Ask around. Consider the options. Don't buy anything on an impulse. But if it's the right decision, go for it.

Checking the List

Non-ownership is a beautiful thing. The less you have, the less you have to take care of. The answer to your question on whether to spend the cash on something may come down to this: Will this purchase be an investment in stuff or an investment in people?

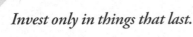 *Invest only in things that last.*

More Veggies

This author recently got diagnosed with type 2 diabetes. I'm not really surprised. It runs in the family. Over the years, three of my grandparents, both parents, and all three siblings received the same diagnosis.

I'm choosing to receive it as good news. Now I have no choice but to get a little more exercise, watch my diet, lose a few pounds, and pay a little more attention to what my body is telling me. I'm still taking in the facts and adjusting my lifestyle. Most of the treatment is common sense, but the last few weeks have brought a few surprises. Especially when it comes to some dos and don'ts.

Thankfully, I can still have my morning black coffee. But orange juice—one of my favorite things in the world—is pretty much forbidden. The sugar content is way too high. For diabetics, the natural sugar in OJ is just as bad as added sugar. Who knew? Of course, I haven't had any soda or candy bars since the diagnosis. Pizza was also put on the restricted list, but I think the best approach for me might be to have one or two slices instead of four or five. I did splurge on a half piece of cake to celebrate my daughter-in-law's birthday. I also sneaked a couple oatmeal cookies while no one was watching. Who was I kidding?

The good news is that mixed nuts, guacamole, fresh salsa, tomato juice, and steel-cut oatmeal are all diabetic friendly. White flour, processed foods, trans fat, and added sugars do the most damage.

So what does all this mean for God's shopping list? It's pretty obvious.

Think about what God gave Adam and Eve to eat in the Garden of Eden. He warned them to stay away from one tree, but the others were fully endorsed: "Then God said, 'I give you every seed-bearing plant on the face of the whole earth and every tree that has fruit with seed in it. They will be yours for food'" (Genesis 1:29). According to the very first chapter of the Bible, whole grains and fresh fruits and vegetables should overflow in our shopping carts.

Consider also that Jesus's first recruits were fishermen. He even facilitated a record-breaking catch that almost sank two boats. Moments later, Jesus did call Peter, James, and John out of the fishing business, but not because it was unhealthy. He had something much better planned, promising to make them "fishers of men" (Matthew 4:19 ESV). Their honorable profession leads me to agree with my new nutritionist, who has already told me that seafood is almost always a good dining option.

She also told me to drink plenty of water. The woman at the well heard the same advice. Even if it was in a little different context.

Here's the takeaway. Your health is important. Your body is a resource given by God. Keeping physically fit allows you to carry God's love to the world. To walk across the street to speak truth to a neighbor. To reach out and hug a hurting friend. To give a cup of cold water. To help carry someone's cross. To run the race set out before you.

To be clear, I know the Bible often uses metaphors. Peter was not being called to literally fish for humans. To the adulterous woman at the well, Jesus was offering not H_2O but living spiritual water. The race we are called to run doesn't require me to go out and pick up a new pair of Nikes.

However, our bodies—as well as our souls—have great value to

God. Sure, our bones and flesh are temporary, but we have a responsibility to stay in shape and stay out of mischief that might compromise our health. Consider 1 Corinthians 6:19-20 (NLT): "Don't you realize that your body is the temple of the Holy Spirit, who lives in you and was given to you by God? You do not belong to yourself, for God bought you with a high price. So you must honor God with your body."

In what other ways can we honor God with our bodies? Assuming a submissive posture when we pray. Getting routine medical screenings. Reserving sex for a committed marriage relationship. Limiting alcohol intake. Refraining from drugs and tobacco. All honorable goals.

If you're doing pretty well in these areas, join me in my next seasons of life. Simply stated, fewer cheeseburgers and more veggies.

Checking the List

I'm not sure we have to go to specialty health food stores or invest in custom diet plans or food delivery services. We all have a sense when we're eating too much of the wrong stuff. Our bodies tell us when we're filling them with poison. Just ten days into an exercise program, we know we'll start feeling stronger and energized. In many ways, our health is not about us. It's about being our best selves so we can serve God and others.

 Honor God with your body.

44

The Pilgrim's Progress, Mere Christianity, The Screwtape Letters, More Than a Carpenter, The Five Love Languages, and So On

I'm glad you're reading this book. It's designed to get you thinking about what's really important and where to invest your resources. Not just money but also how to maximize your time and effort. Hopefully, it's also challenging you to see that your talents, spiritual gifts, and life experience are gifts from God that he has given specifically to you to use wisely and give glory back to him.

This author and my publisher have high hopes for this book. But honestly, there's really only a slim chance that it will become a classic.

With that in mind, we recommend you check the following Christian classics off your shopping list (once you finish this book). If you already have, that's great. Go ahead and skip to the next chapter in this book.

Pilgrim's Progress. Presented as a dream, this entertaining allegory by John Bunyan follows an everyman character named Christian in his formidable journey from the City of Destruction to the Celestial City. A slew of helpful, dangerous, and distracting characters cross his path, including Mr. Worldly Wiseman, Faithful, Hopeful, Envy, Obstinate, Giant Despair, and the Flatterer. Will he make it through the Wicket Gate and the Enchanted Ground? A 1678 classic, *Pilgrim's Progress* is one of the bestselling books of all time and has been revised by several publishers.

Mere Christianity. This 1952 book from one of the most important writers of the twentieth century is predominantly transcripts from BBC radio talks by C.S. Lewis between 1941 and 1944. Concerned that World War II was breaking the spirit of the British people, the BBC director of religious broadcasting asked Lewis to provide spiritual comfort, direction, and practical application of biblical truth via a series of radio broadcasts. The book is fun to read and makes complex spiritual concepts accessible without watering them down or talking down to the reader.

The Screwtape Letters. Also by C.S. Lewis, this imaginative allegory invites readers to follow a series of letters written by one of Satan's senior demons, Uncle Screwtape, to his nephew Wormwood. The satirical perspective offers advice on how to tempt, manipulate, and distract humans to win their souls for hell. The book's upside-down world presents light as darkness, virtue as weakness, and God as the Enemy. Brilliant.

More Than a Carpenter. Renowned apologist Josh McDowell describes this book as everything he would want to say to a skeptic or seeking friend over a cup of coffee. In less than 130 pages, Josh delivers almost a dozen commonsense and intellectually sound reasons to believe Jesus really is the Son of God and to trust the resurrection, as well as a helpful explanation of how lives are changed when people accept Christ as their Savior. With more than 30 million copies in print in more than 100 languages, *More Than a Carpenter* may be the most powerful evangelism tool ever created.

The Five Love Languages. For good reason, this book and its spinoffs have sold a gazillion copies. Even if you've read it, you'll want to go back and consider how it applies to all your changing relationships.

Gary Chapman encourages you to be intentional about deciphering the love languages of all the people in your life who matter to you. By knowing whether their love language is words of affirmation, quality time, receiving gifts, acts of service, or physical touch, you will better serve and communicate with them.

Yes, the Bible is the very first item on God's reading list for you. But he has also gifted phenomenal writers, teachers, and theologians to give you a fresh look at how the Bible applies to life. There is a place for allegories, relationship manuals, commentaries, Christian fiction, devotionals, and children's books.

Ask the people in your life who made it through a stormy season or seem to have their act together, "What's your favorite book?" "Can you recommend a good book to help me face a challenge?" More times than not, it will be a Christian classic by someone like Josh McDowell or C.S. Lewis.

Checking the List

The five classics mentioned in this chapter are personal favorites. Your friends will have their own. And so will you. If you're going through a dry spell or want to turn your faith up a notch, it's never a bad idea to go back to the classics. Talk about them. Read and reread them. You'll find something new each time. Hey, that's why they're classics.

Read Christian classics.

45

Piano, Art Easel, Wrestling Mat, Unicycle

This chapter is specifically for parents. Moms and dads face a constant struggle between pushing our kids to meet their potential versus backing off and letting them be kids. So what might be on God's shopping list that would help you stay in balance?

On one hand, you don't want to burden your children with adult responsibilities and pressures. That will all come soon enough. On the other hand, if you can identify their gifts and passions early, your kids have a better chance of doing great things in life.

That's why supportive parents put a piano in the corner of their living room to give their kids a shot at becoming the next Beethoven, Billy Joel, or Michael W. Smith. They buy an art easel and paints, which may lead to a child becoming a modern-day Rembrandt or Michelangelo. They lay out a wrestling mat in the basement, envisioning their son as a state champion wrestler. They buy a unicycle for a middle-schooler just because it would be cool to watch them do something that looks impossible.

I did all those things. And what happened?

In some ways, it doesn't matter what happened. Because our job as parents is to open doors for our kids. Let them try piano, painting, wrestling, and unicycling. Start them off with a little instruction. Be a cheerleader. Set them up for an early taste of success if possible. And then let them decide. Each child will choose to walk through that open door or not. The goal is to push them just enough and know when to stop. Or know when to keep nudging them forward.

Often, the results are unexpected. Events over which you have zero control. Maybe no one in your house becomes a concert pianist, but the kid down the street sits down and starts noodling on your piano, which leads to your daughter becoming a jazz vocalist. Maybe no masterpieces are painted on that art easel, but the family uses it regularly to play Pictionary, and one of your kids becomes a motivational speaker or game-show host. Maybe your son never gets enthusiastic about wrestling, but your young daughter starts tumbling on that mat and becomes a world-class gymnast. Maybe that unicycle hangs in your garage for years, but one day an older teen pulls it down and masters the one-wheeled beast. Then joins the circus! Wouldn't that be weird and wonderful?

An investment in your kids is an investment in the future. It doesn't always work out the way you planned it in your head, and there are no guarantees. Your job is to accept them as a gift, enjoy every season you have with them, and then let them go.

Psalm 127:3-4 (NLT) provides a great image for parents: "Children are a gift from the Lord; they are a reward from him. Children born to a young man are like arrows in a warrior's hands." That portion of Scripture suggests your job as a steadfast archer is to stand firm, sharpen your arrows, help them choose the right target (which is different for every child), hold them close to your heart, and let them fly. What a privilege that is!

By the way, that piano, art easel, wrestling mat, and unicycle can also be used by grown-ups. If you're raising kids—exposing them to new options and experiences—don't be surprised if you take on some new challenges yourself.

If there are no youngsters in your life right now, that gives you even more reasons to stretch yourself and try new things. Keep opening doors for yourself and everyone in your life.

Checking the List

When was the last time you tried something new? Not dangerous. Not wasteful. Not immoral. Just something you happen to stumble across in the course of life. Or something you've been considering for quite a while. Open that door. Walk through on your own or with someone you care about.

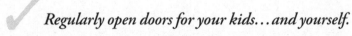 *Regularly open doors for your kids...and yourself.*

That Thing You Need
Before You Run Out

Consider all the things you need in the course of a day. Not big things, like your car or refrigerator, but little things you often take for granted. Specifically, those relatively inexpensive items you don't want to run out of, or your day will take a disappointing turn.

You know the feeling. You reach for it and it's not there. The productivity you hoped to enjoy for the next hour or so pretty much grinds to a halt. Maybe it takes you by surprise, or maybe you knew you were running low. In any case, your mood takes a nasty turn. And your options are limited.

Suddenly, your next activity is driving across town to purchase a single item. Or you find yourself placing a rush order online and paying for same-day delivery. Or maybe you are left uncomfortable, undernourished, or unkempt for the day.

What kind of things are we talking about? Toothpaste, shampoo, deodorant, milk, bread, eggs, coffee, coffee filters, sandwich bags, toilet paper, clean underwear, clean socks, printer ink cartridges, printer paper, packing tape, AA batteries, gas for your lawnmower, garbage bags, business cards, furnace filters, vacuum cleaner bags, lightbulbs, water softener salt, sunblock, dishwashing liquid, laundry detergent, fabric softener, and dog food.

You'll notice that you can't fake most things on this list. When you're out, you're out. Sure, if you have plastic wrap, you can pack a lunch without sandwich bags. Dogs can live on table scraps for a day. You can move a lightbulb from a noncritical location to a lamp you need to use right now. You can sometimes coax a few more copies out of a printer cartridge by giving it a good shake. But let's all agree that it's much easier to have all these things on hand before you run out.

That's why all those items are on God's shopping list for your life. Does God really care about the items in your pantry, bathroom cabinet, or storage closet? Well, not directly. He knows the things of this world are temporary. But he does care about you. He cares about your resources—your time, talent, and treasure. He wants you to make the most of your gifts and to focus less on stuff and more on him.

That's right, the Creator of the universe cares about every detail of your life. Right down to your eyelashes. Luke 12:7 makes the incredible affirmation that "the very hairs of your head are all numbered." That's how well God knows you and cares about you. So it's not a stretch of the imagination to say he knows when your printer ink is running low and doesn't want you to lose your cool or lose a client when you can't finish printing out that 143-page report.

So do yourself a favor and anticipate the dwindling supply of all these things—and anything else you can think of. Don't stockpile a year's worth of everything. But don't wait until the last minute or until you're down to the last ounce, sip, sheet, squirt, bulb, battery, or bag. You'll save trips to the store and wangle the best bargains if you give yourself a little time.

One last thought. If you happen to be working on a project for a church or ministry and you run out of ink, tape, foam core, construction paper, or glue sticks, there are some people who might blame Satanic influence. I understand that concept. Satan absolutely hates seeing followers of Christ get together in an organized effort to worship, teach, evangelize, and pray. He's got more power and influence than most people think. On any given Sunday, his scheme for the morning may be for the kindergarten classroom to run out of green felt a week before Christmas. That could be the case. But really, isn't it more likely that someone in charge of supplies simply forgot to place that order for green felt?

Coming full circle, do yourself a favor and stay on guard against memory lapses and short shipping deadlines. Give yourself some margin. Look for stock-up sales. When you run out of something, mobilize your common sense and ingenuity to rescue the day.

But don't beat up on yourself if you run out of deodorant, coffee filters, or garbage bags. It's not the end of the world. There are many more important things with which to concern yourself. Like staying vigilant for real attacks from the evil one. And preparing for the real end of the world.

Checking the List

When facing those inevitable, teeny-tiny frustrations of life, let's pledge to turn it down a notch. When facing life-or-death challenges or the darkest forces of the spiritual world, let's pledge to turn to God in prayer and allow him to lead us with our very best efforts and attention to detail.

 Stay vigilant. Build margin into your life and schedule. Focus on what's really important.

Tickets

I understand why you're not racing to the local Cineplex to see the latest Hollywood blockbuster or excited about seeing the latest Broadway musical. And it's not just the rising price of tickets and popcorn.

Much of today's so-called entertainment is violent, depressing, graphic, filthy, angry, and hopeless. The themes run counter to your values. The Broadway show that used to deliver tunes celebrating life and elevating audiences now often glorifies the dark side of life. Even something described by critics as the "feel-good movie of the year" features a climactic scene in which the main characters make terrible decisions.

There's no end in sight to the slippery slope. Every generation seems to sink to a new low of what they consider acceptable. Even worse than the obvious assault on our senses may be the subtle systematic perversion of our worldview. In the name of tolerance, any choice made by anyone onstage or on-screen is not to be judged.

Frankly, we shouldn't be surprised. Protecting values is not the responsibility of film studios and theater producers. They are just doing their job. Their assignment is to make as much money as possible for their companies. If they don't believe in God, why would they follow a biblical worldview when selecting scripts?

So then, how can God-fearing patrons convince producers there is a better option than creating more garbage, lies, and half-truths? Maybe by using our pocketbooks.

Many of today's films and theater options will drag you down, but some new releases value what you value. Seek them out. Talk to like-minded friends. Read reviews. Read between the lines of reviews. Do your research. Be a little skeptical of film critics, trailers, and even the movie ratings from the Motion Picture Association of America. Critics are often part of the revisionist agenda. Trailers cunningly leave out controversial material to lure unsuspecting patrons. Movie ratings are assigned by Hollywood insiders who rarely share your values. Your best bet is to seek out websites sponsored by organizations like the Dove Foundation and Plugged In. They can help uncover any unsavory agenda a film might be advancing.

When you find a movie with a positive message, you know what to do. Buy a ticket. That should include quality films produced by the major studios as well as the latest releases from Christian filmmakers like Pure Flix, Affirm Films, Walden Media, Franklin Entertainment, ODB Films, and the Kendrick Brothers. The good news is that Hollywood has recently seen an increase in profits distributing films with Christian themes. Your ticket purchases will keep that trend growing.

As for Broadway and their touring shows, I know they can't all be *Les Misérables*, and we don't need to go back to the innocent days of *Oklahoma!* and *Guys and Dolls*. But the goal should be to enjoy musicals that don't leave us wincing, covering the eyes and ears of our youngsters in the next seat, and feeling like we have to take a bath to wash off the stink. Naming specific musicals would be counterproductive, so we'll leave it at that. Except to reiterate that when you find a well-done, uplifting show, tell your friends and head for the box office.

The answer to which film and stage productions get your entertainment dollar may be found in the passage of Scripture that reads, "Finally, brothers and sisters, whatever is true, whatever is noble, whatever is right, whatever is pure, whatever is lovely, whatever is admirable—if anything is excellent or praiseworthy—think about such things" (Philippians 4:8).

Does that sound like a plan? What if we all encouraged our family and friends to open their hearts and minds (and wallets) only to things that are noble, pure, lovely, admirable, excellent, and praiseworthy? Then more of those kinds of productions would get made. It's simple economics.

By the way, if you didn't know, website analytics and cookies are currently tracking all your internet activities, including search engine queries, sites visited, online purchases, and even the movements of your mouse across a webpage. You've been warned.

Here's the point. Your ticket purchases, web browsing, listening habits, Facebook comments, and much more impact the decisions made by entertainment producers. So you have more power and influence than you might think. These days, whatever you seek, you'll get more of. Let's pledge to seek, find, and buy the stuff that makes this world a kinder, gentler, more God-honoring place.

Checking the List

You have to question the label "adult audiences" regarding softcore porn, extreme lifestyle choices, and über-violence. Sure, we need to protect our kids from images and ideas they can't handle. But really, should we adults be letting that stuff into our own heads? Let's not hide from the world, but let's use our influence to make our preferences known.

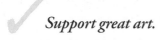 *Support great art.*

Lottery Tickets

I suppose that if you buy one lottery ticket once in a while just for fun, it's not the worst thing in the world.

But I have to say that in my humble opinion, the government-run lottery is a scam, a land mine, a distraction, and a national tragedy. Let me spell it out.

Scam. Millionaires don't play the lottery. Just the opposite. People living in or close to poverty are the most frequent buyers of lottery tickets. A recent study titled "Gambling on the Lottery: Sociodemographic Correlates Across the Lifespan" published in the *Journal of Gambling Studies* found the "highest rate of lottery gambling (61%) and the highest mean level of days gambled in the past year" were exhibited in the population in the lowest fifth in terms of socioeconomic status. [5] In other words, the people who can least afford to play are playing.

What's more, the initial claim in many state-run lotteries was that the profits would be used to support education. In truth, the money spent on education is rarely linked to lottery activity.

Land mine. Even the winners don't really win. They become targets for con men, high-risk investments, and friends and relatives looking for a handout. The National Endowment for Financial Education estimates that up to 70 percent of Americans who win a lottery or experience a sudden windfall lose that money within a few years.

Distraction. Winning the lottery—even just playing the lottery—takes your eyes off Jesus. He should be our source of hope, not some bouncing numbered balls falling into a random slot. We need to get up in the morning thinking, *How can I know and serve Jesus better today?*, not *Will I win the lottery?*

For many people, playing the lottery—or really any gambling—is a crippling life focus. They become slaves to standing in line at the quick mart or watching wide-eyed as the numbers are chosen. Matthew 6:24 speaks to that kind of bondage: "No one can serve two masters. Either you will hate the one and love the other, or you will be devoted to the one and despise the other."

What's more, a survey by Consumer Federation of America found that 30 percent of Americans without a high school degree said winning the lottery was a "very important wealth-building strategy."[6] I wonder if budgeting, saving, job training, and hard work were other strategies being considered.

National tragedy. According to CNN Money, Americans spend more than $70 billion per year on lottery tickets alone. That's more than the total spending on music, books, sports teams, movies, and video games combined.[7] Supposedly, the income from the lottery reduces our taxes. But maybe it's actually raising government expenses. Really, there's no way to know how playing the lottery demotivates our citizens, drives more Americans to welfare, and leads to other societal ills, such as depression, divorce, crime, and excess consumer debt.

Proverbs has a great bit of wisdom to consider when addressing the topic of the lottery or any path toward easy money: "Wealth from get-rich-quick schemes quickly disappears; wealth from hard work grows over time" (Proverbs 13:11 NLT).

Checking the List

When a big payout is due on the national lottery, inevitably the local news station sends a reporter to the mini-mart around the corner to ask lottery players, "What would you do if you hit the jackpot?" I always feel a little sorry for those people. Don't you?

 Know the source of true riches.

The Full Armor

If God wrote your shopping list, he would want you to arm yourself for the inevitable spiritual battles you will face. That includes flesh-and-blood enemies commissioned by Satan and invisible forces too horrible to imagine. Neither can be defeated alone.

In our broken world, visible evildoers may include playground bullies, drug dealers, sexual predators, human traffickers, terrorists, and serial killers. Those adversaries are not subtle; we know when we're under attack. Others may do their damage in less obvious ways. Friends who betray you. Coworkers who slander you. Unrepentant sinners who do not appreciate you seeking God's will for your life. Perhaps worst of all, those who pretend to speak for God but are doing just the opposite.

Then there are invisible demons. Their goal is straightforward—to separate Christians from God. Their strategy is to glorify sin. They tempt, scheme, accuse, deceive, and mock believers. In many cases, the closer you are to God, the harder they work to make you doubt.

That's why the apostle Paul gives this unmistakable command:

> Put on the full armor of God, so that you can take your stand against the devil's schemes. For our struggle is not against flesh and blood, but against the rulers, against

the authorities, against the powers of this dark world and against the spiritual forces of evil in the heavenly realms. Therefore put on the full armor of God, so that when the day of evil comes, you may be able to stand your ground, and after you have done everything, to stand. Stand firm then, with the belt of truth buckled around your waist, with the breastplate of righteousness in place, and with your feet fitted with the readiness that comes from the gospel of peace. In addition to all this, take up the shield of faith, with which you can extinguish all the flaming arrows of the evil one. Take the helmet of salvation and the sword of the Spirit, which is the word of God (Ephesians 6:11-17).

The armor of God is a not a myth or a joke; it's a metaphor for all we must do to prepare for battle. When my kids were young, they had a gray-and-gold plastic play set of the armor of God. Not sure where it came from. This predated Amazon, so it's quite possible I happened to see it at a Christian bookstore. Actually, they're still readily available online. As a teaching tool, they're fine. But make no mistake, this is life-and-death stuff. What's more, we are not instructed to just pick up one or two components of this battle gear. We need to implement the "full armor of God."

The belt of truth sets us free. Knowing truth opens our eyes to God's power, love, and grace. Speaking and living the truth prevents us from opening the door to Satan's lies.

The breastplate of righteousness protects our heart. We can claim to be righteous only because of God's grace. Our justification by the blood of Christ means the very core of who we are has been transformed—made new—and nothing can separate us from God's love. He is our bulletproof vest.

The sandals of peace allow us to walk with Jesus. We are sure-footed, no longer stumbling in the dark. We can stand secure, ready to defend our faith with the gospel and give a reason for the hope we have.

The shield of faith blocks every flaming arrow Satan fires. Be aware—on our own, we lose. But our faith in God gives us courage to face the enemy. Even more important, God's faithfulness makes that shield impenetrable.

The helmet of salvation protects our mind. Salvation is not just a feeling, it's a decision we make to trust Christ. We can make that choice only when we come to an understanding of our sinful condition, the destination we deserve (hell), the power of Jesus's love, the free gift of grace that pays the price for our sins, and our dependence on that most generous gift because we couldn't do anything to save ourselves.

The sword of the Spirit—the Bible—is our most powerful weapon, sharpening us and warding off Satan every time we read from it. Matthew 4:4 recalls how Jesus was tempted by Satan in the desert. The Son of God could have called on a legion of angels to rescue him, but instead he quoted Scripture, and that was enough to defeat Satan. "Jesus answered, 'It is written: "Man shall not live on bread alone, but on every word that comes from the mouth of God."'" It's worth remembering, you and I have that same weapon. Let's keep it sharp.

The full armor of God doesn't have a price tag. But we have a clear directive and undeniable motivation to put all six battle-ready armaments on our shopping list.

Checking the List

God has already defeated Satan. But the prince of darkness still has power over us mere mortals. That's why we need to make our allegiance clear. "Submit yourselves, then, to God. Resist the devil, and he will flee from you" (James 4:7).

 Implement God's surefire plan to defeat Satan.

Gold Bricks

D id you hear the story about the wealthy man who prayed so earnestly that Saint Peter granted his wish and agreed to let him bring one suitcase of whatever he wanted into heaven?

The man filled his largest trunk with gold bars and upon his death dragged it confidently up to the pearly gates. After some brief paperwork, Saint Peter opened the trunk to inspect the worldly items the man found too precious to leave behind and exclaimed, "You brought pavement?"

It's a good joke. Feel free to put it in your good-joke arsenal and tell it anytime the topic of gold, pavement, Saint Peter, the celestial city, or the pearly gates comes up.

If you don't get it, you'll want to look up Revelation 21, in which John describes the new eternal earth that awaits those whose names are written in the book of life. After chronicling the millennium, Satan's final demise, and the judgment of the dead, John gives some amazing specifics regarding the New Jerusalem. That includes a city with walls made of precious jewels and gates of pearl. The punchline of the joke appears in verse 21 (NLT): "The main street was pure gold."

On one hand, the joke is a reminder of the place that God has prepared for us. There's no way the human mind can imagine it. "No eye has seen, no ear has heard, and no mind has imagined what God has prepared for those who love him" (1 Corinthians 2:9 NLT).

In other words, John used the most superlative words he could find to describe heaven, but he couldn't even come close to the overwhelming beauty and magnificence of what's waiting for believers. It's way better than crystal, jewels, and gold.

On the other hand, the joke is a warning to those who believe that wealth here on earth is the ultimate goal. There is no debate on that point. Jesus's words are clear: "I tell you, it is easier for a camel to go through the eye of a needle than for someone who is rich to enter the kingdom of God" (Matthew 19:24).

All joking aside, gold bricks are certainly not on God's shopping list for your life. The more you have, the tougher it is to let go of them. The more you have, the greater distraction they are to what's really important. Consider yourself warned.

What *is* on your shopping list is hope. Hope from the one source.

> Command those who are rich in this present world not to be arrogant nor to put their hope in wealth, which is so uncertain, but to put their hope in God, who richly provides us with everything for our enjoyment. Command them to do good, to be rich in good deeds, and to be generous and willing to share. In this way they will lay up treasure for themselves as a firm foundation for the coming age, so that they may take hold of the life that is truly life (1 Timothy 6:17-19).

Be rich in good deeds. Be generous and willing to share. Those will be part of your firm foundation for the future, sturdier than any bricks of gold.

Checking the List

Just to be clear, wealth and money on their own are not the problem.

Hard work should be rewarded. The wise use of money can be a blessing to others. Taking care of your family is a biblical responsibility. Money is not evil. According to 1 Timothy 6:10 (NLT), "The love of money is the root of all kinds of evil."

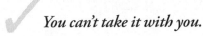 *You can't take it with you.*

Sunday Brunch

If you've got kids, family members, houseguests, friends, or a spouse who doesn't jump out of bed with enthusiasm on some Sunday mornings, this might be one of the most valuable items on God's shopping list for you.

It's not a long-term solution, but I think it's perfectly okay to use Sunday brunch as a way to lure children and adults to Sunday service. Can you relate?

(Let's also confess that sometimes, one of the reasons you and I have the gumption to get out of bed on Sunday is because we're looking forward to a nice omelet or sweet stack of French toast after service.)

Of course, if you've been part of the same church family for a while, the worship, message, fellowship, and movement of the Spirit often launches your week in amazing, even miraculous ways. Going to church can and should be a blessing! It provides courage and encouragement. You interact with dear friends who have meant so much over the years, standing with you through personal tragedies and during moments of joyful celebration. You sing praise songs to the Creator of the universe, who is worthy and appreciative. Scripture is read right out loud, which means you hear direct quotations from God that apply to your life this very day.

Even the building is important to you. You recall a conversation in that corner of the lobby when a member of your small group helped pray you through a dark time. Down that hallway, you volunteered in children's ministry and were privileged to impact young lives. Down the center aisle in the sanctuary, you walked beside the casket of a dear one who died too young. Outside the front doors, you threw rice or birdseed, blew bubbles, or waved sparklers as a fresh-faced young couple began their life together. Just walking into the community center fills you with memories of potlucks, Christmas teas, youth-group shenanigans, and outreach projects that led to lives being changed in your community or the other side of the world.

For the most part, you rarely doubt the value of investing a Sunday morning at church. But sometimes—especially after a late Saturday night—it's not easy to get up and go. Besides, it really is okay to miss sometimes. It's not a sin to miss a Sunday service.

That's where Sunday brunch comes in. When you whip up a spectacular smorgasbord at home or fill a table at the local pancake house, you are actually keeping the celebration going! Talk about the sermon. Ooh and aah over the scribbly Sunday-school art projects of the preschoolers. Join hands for a short, humble prayer of thanks and blessing just after the food arrives.

To increase your chance of maximum participation, make a brief announcement to the home crowd Saturday evening. "Hey, let's hit the ten o'clock service tomorrow and go for brunch afterward." Don't make it a question. Assume 100 percent participation. That should get everyone in the household on board, and it gives you permission to start knocking on doors the next morning at the appropriate time. You can even send a similar text or email out to that one person you've been thinking about inviting to church. Mention the sermon topic and the free brunch, and then add, "Thought you might like to join us."

I'm thinking the Bible is filled with all kinds of lessons learned before, after, and during meals. I'm pretty sure that's why God created brunch.

Checking the List

During a service, how often have you thought this? *I wish my sister/son/neighbor/coworker/schoolmate were here today. They would have really appreciated this message.* An invitation to brunch is a practical and valuable tool you can use to increase the attendance at and longevity of your Sunday celebration.

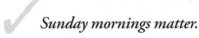 *Sunday mornings matter.*

Contentment

Let's finish the shopping list God might have for our lives with one more item that isn't for sale at any price: contentment. What is it? How do we get it?

Contentment is not synonymous with happiness or pleasure. By necessity, those are temporary conditions. Sadness will enter your life, and that's not a bad thing. After a significant loss, the only way to regain your strength and balance is to endure a period of grief and mourning. And consider the occasions of your greatest pleasure. If extreme pleasure never ended, it would lead to madness.

Neither is contentment about possessing everything you could ever want. If you find yourself on a quest for more, by definition it would never end. Socrates is often quoted as saying, "He who is not contented with what he has would not be contented with what he would like to have."[8]

Also, contentment cannot be about comparing yourself with your neighbor. Their needs, motivations, giftedness, and deepest desires have nothing to do with you. Besides, the tenth commandment is quite clear: "You shall not covet your neighbor's house. You shall not covet your neighbor's wife, or his male or female servant, his ox or donkey, or anything that belongs to your neighbor" (Exodus 20:17).

No amount of cash will guarantee contentment. As a matter of fact, the more you have, the more you have to worry about. Worry is the opposite of contentment.

Contentment is about seeing God for who he is—an awesome Creator who cares about each one of us on a personal level. "Better a little with the fear of the LORD than great wealth with turmoil" (Proverbs 15:16).

Said another way, contentment is about living in God's sweet spot. Trusting him. Seeing the big picture. Knowing that this season of plenty or want will not last. And that's okay.

God modeled contentment in the attitude displayed by Paul in the last chapter of the book of Philippians. Writing from a prison cell, Paul was expressing gratitude to a group of believers in Philippi who had sent him a gift. In addition to thanking them, he wanted to let them know he was rejoicing in his relationship with Christ in good times and in bad.

> I have learned how to be content with whatever I have. I know how to live on almost nothing or with everything. I have learned the secret of living in every situation, whether it is with a full stomach or empty, with plenty or little. For I can do everything through Christ, who gives me strength (Philippians 4:11-13 NLT).

It may be an overstatement, but God wants you to experience Paul's secret. To live it out in your life. To be able to face imprisonment and even death with a sense of contentment. Is that something you can do?

In a book about shopping, it may seem strange to make the following challenge. But I invite you to spend just a few minutes exploring your home, office, yard, bookshelves, workbench, bedrooms, and garage. Consider all your stuff. Every cherished object. Every ridiculous impulse buy you made. The stuff that maxed out your credit card. The stuff you prayed about before purchasing. Lay eyes on every piece.

Or simply imagine the accumulation of stuff over the years. Then realize it will all be dust sooner rather than later. Less than dust.

There can be no contentment there. No fulfillment. No purpose. Again, if it hasn't been clear, hang on to this truth one more time. Life is about relationship, not stuff. Relationship with people in your life— from strangers to loved ones. Relationship with the Father, Son, and Holy Spirit. The Creator, the Savior, the Counselor.

That's where you will find contentment. Look for it; you'll find it right in front of you. And your heart will overflow with gratitude and love.

Checking the List

Put the credit card down. Stop buying things. Clear the clutter. At the same time, call your mom. Engage your dad. Text your teenager. Wave to a neighbor. Hug a friend. Thank a veteran. Forgive an old wound. Speak kindness to a stranger. Spend time with the Creator—in prayer or just resting in contentment for all he has done.

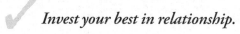 *Invest your best in relationship.*

Notes

1. Adapted in part from Jay Payleitner, *52 Things Kids Need from a Dad* (Eugene: Harvest House, 2010), 65-67.

2. Adapted from Jay Payleitner, *52 Things to Pray for Your Kids* (Eugene: Harvest House, 2015), 65-67.

3. Adapted from Jay Payleitner, *52 Things to Pray for Your Kids* (Eugene: Harvest House, 2015), 175-77.

4. Neal D. Fortin, *Food Regulation: Law, Science, Policy, and Practice* (Hoboken, NJ: Wiley, 2007), 153-54.

5. Cited in John Wihbey, "Who Plays the Lottery, and Why: Updated Collection of Research," *Journalist's Resource*, July 27, 2016, https://journalistsresource.org/studies/economics/personal-finance/research-review-lotteries-demographics.

6. "How Americans View Personal Wealth vs. How Financial Planners View This Wealth," Consumer Federation of America and the Financial Planning Association, January 9, 2006, https://consumerfed.org/pdfs/Financial_Planners_Study011006.pdf.

7. Amelia Josephson, "The Economics of the Lottery," *SmartAsset*, June 18, 2018, https://smartasset.com/taxes/the-economics-of-the-lottery.

8. The quote is actually a variant of a few of Socrates's other quotes, but it sounds like something he would have said, doesn't it?

About the Author

Jay Payleitner is one of the top freelance producers for Christian radio. For more than a decade, Jay produced *Josh McDowell Radio, Today's Father, Jesus Freaks Radio,* and *Project Angel Tree* with Chuck Colson.

Jay is a longtime affiliate with the National Center for Fathering and nationally known motivational speaker for Iron Sharpens Iron, marriage conferences, outreach events, and weekend services. Jay has sold more than a half million books, including the bestselling *52 Things Kids Need from a Dad, What If God Wrote Your Bucket List?,* and *The Jesus Dare.* Jay's books have been translated into French, German, Spanish, Afrikaans, Indonesian, Slovenian, and Russian. He has been a guest multiple times on *The Harvest Show, 100 Huntley Street,* and *Focus on the Family.*

Jay and his high school sweetheart, Rita, live in the Chicago area, where they've raised five great kids, loved on ten foster babies, and are cherishing grandparenthood.

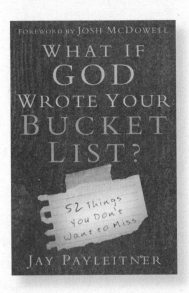

What If God Wrote Your Bucket List?

Go bungee jumping. Tango. See the Eiffel Tower. Swim with sharks.

Bucket lists can get pretty crazy! But what if God wanted you to think even further outside the box? To pattern your life after the one who said some pretty crazy things himself: "Love your enemies." "Store up treasures in heaven." "Seek first his kingdom and righteousness."

If you checked every item off your bucket list, would your life be complete? In these pages you'll find 52 items to help you revamp your must-do list...

- Run with scissors. Bounce off brick walls. Celebrate quirks.
- Banish grudges. Dodge counterfeit happiness. Peek into dark corners.
- Get fired. Enlist invisible reinforcements. Get nose-to-nose with an alligator.

As you check off God's bucket list, you may find yourself doing things you never thought possible. Jay Payleitner helps you get your priorities straight with the most important relationship in your life—you and God.

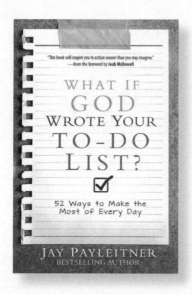

What If God Wrote Your To-Do List?

What is God asking you to do today?

When you talk to God about his plans for you, do you tend to focus on the far-off future? Big-picture thinking is great, but don't miss out on what the Lord has in store for you today.

These 52 user-friendly tasks will help you embrace opportunities to grow closer to God, reach out to others, and take better care of yourself. This is a to-do list for your soul.

Read a psalm, eat the frog, draw in the sand, or buy a used tuxedo. It's amazing how a few inspired activities can renew and enrich your everyday life.

God is calling you to make the most of each day and live life to the fullest!

More Great Harvest House Books by Jay Payleitner

52 Ways to Connect as a Couple
In these 52 short readings, popular author and speaker Jay Payleitner addresses head-on some of the obstacles to oneness and suggests out-of-the-box solutions for overcoming them. Sometimes spiritual, sometimes silly, but always practical, winsome, and wise, these ideas will help you connect and make your marriage better than ever.

52 Things Husbands Need from Their Wives
Jay digs deep to give practical, doable, fun, and unexpected ideas for a wife to connect with her husband by listening, remembering he's a man, encouraging him with her words, making space for him to participate, respecting him, and appreciating his "hero moments." Great steps for strengthening a marriage!

52 Things Wives Need from Their Husbands
For the husband who wants to live out God's plan for his marriage, *52 Things Wives Need from Their Husbands* provides a full year's worth of advice that will put you on the right track without making you feel guilty or criticizing you for acting like a man. A great gift or men's group resource.

The Dad Book
Jay has packed this handy volume full of quick, inspiring help:
- fresh suggestions for engaging your kids
- dad-to-dad humor
- ways to *show* your kids instead of *tell* them
- encouragement and ideas to help your kids connect with God

A great confidence-booster for dads of any age and stage!

The Dad Manifesto
This pocket-size collection of tips, tricks, and tidbits provides the inspiration you need to become the best dad you can be. Each page features a fun project, a creative experience, or an important commitment that will help you establish a connection with your kids that will last a lifetime.

365 Ways to Say "I Love You" to Your Kids
You adore your kids, but expressions of love can get lost in the mayhem of daily living. Jay inspires you to show your affection, pride, and joy with 365 simple ideas that will encourage and nurture your child one loving moment at a time.

52 Things to Pray for Your Kids
How do you raise your kids up into godly young adults? Jay knows the power of sustained prayer over his children. With surprising insight into praying for your children's health, safety, and character, this resource will help you pray powerfully for *and with* children of any age.

10 Conversations Kids Need to Have with Their Dad
Straightforward, man-friendly advice about communicating all-important life values to your kids. Plant healthy thoughts about *excellence, emotions, integrity, marriage, immortality*, and five other key character qualities. A terrific, confidence-boosting resource for building lifelong positives into your family.

52 Things Kids Need from a Dad
Straightforward features with step-up-to-the-mark challenges make this an empowering confidence builder with focu'''doable ideas. Includes expanded insights on some of the rules in *The Dad Manifesto* and iong lists or criticism for acting like a man. Great gift or men's group resource! More ian 150,000 sold.

52 Things Sons Need from Their Dads
These 52 quick-to-read chapters offer a bucketful of man-friendly ideas on building a father-son relationship. By your life and example, you can show your boy how to work hard and have fun, often at the same time; live with honesty and self-respect; and develop the inner confidence to live purposefully.

52 Things Daughters Need from Their Dads
Jay guides you into "girl land," offering ways to do things *with* your daughter, not just *for* her; lecture less and listen more; be alert for "hero moments"; and give your daughter a positive view of the male sex. You'll gain confidence in building lifelong positives into your daughter at every age.

The Little Book of Big Ideas for Dads and Daughters
This one-of-a-kind book features more than 50 fun and practical ways to build a great relationship with your daughter. Find out how you can make a difference in the most important parts of her life, such as her personal faith and relationships.

101 Things Great Dads Do
Being a great father is all about small, consistent steps you can take to creatively love, lead, and teach your kids. This book is packed with 101 dad-doable tasks to help you better connect with your children in simple yet powerful ways.

To learn more about Harvest House books and
to read sample chapters, visit our website:

www.harvesthousepublishers.com

HARVEST HOUSE PUBLISHERS
EUGENE, OREGON